Crafting Cinematic Excellence

Navigating Filmmaking in The Modern Era

By

Joseph Thompson, MFA

Copyright Page: Copyright © 2023 by Joseph Thompson, MFA All rights reserved. No part of this publication may be reproduced, stored in a retrieval system, or transmitted, in any form or by any means, electronic, mechanical, photocopying, recording, or otherwise, without the prior permission of the author.

Dedication

Page Foreword by Joseph Thompson, MFA

To my mother and father, and to my grandparents, Mr. and Mrs. Haynes, who always believed in me and supported me in pursuing my dreams. Thank you for your unwavering love and encouragement.

Acknowledgement:

I would like to express my gratitude to all the people who have contributed to the making of this book. I would like to thank my editor, proofreaders, and everyone who provided feedback and suggestions. Special thanks to my family and friends for their support and understanding throughout the writing process.

Table of Contents

Introduction..1
STORYTELLING...26
DIRECTING..36
CINEAMATOGRAPHY...54
FILM EDITING...68
VARIOUS FORMS OF FILMMAKING....................73
ART DIRECTION..87
INVOKING COLOR IN FILM AND EDITING TECHNIQUES........97
HOW TO CREATE A SAMPLE SCENE AND DIALOGUE FOR A MOVIE162

INTRODUCTION

This book is a comprehensive guide to filmmaking for beginners. Joseph Thompson, MFA, has created a manual that covers all aspects of filmmaking, from directing to screenwriting. Whether you're just starting out or looking to improve your skills, this guide is an invaluable resource. It's a must-read for anyone interested in pursuing a career in the film industry. I highly recommend this book to anyone who wants to learn the ins and outs of filmmaking.

ROLES AND JOBS IN FILM PRODUCTION

There are many different roles involved in film production, and each role has a specific responsibility. Here is an overview of some of the key roles and their responsibilities:

1. **Producer**: The producer is responsible for overseeing the entire production, including raising funds, hiring the director and other key personnel, managing the budget, and ensuring that the project is completed on time and within budget.
2. **Director:** The director is responsible for bringing the script to life on screen. They work with the actors, cinematographer, and other crew members to create the visual style and tone of the film.
3. Screenwriter: The screenwriter is responsible for writing the script for the film. They may work closely with the director and producer to ensure that the script meets their vision for the film.
4. **Cinematographer:** The cinematographer, also known as the director of photography, is responsible for the camera work and lighting of the film. They work closely with the director to create the visual style of the film and oversee the camera and lighting crew.
5. **Production Designer**: The production designer is responsible for the overall look and feel of the film, including sets, costumes, props, and other visual elements.
6. **Editor:** The editor is responsible for assembling the footage into a coherent narrative. They work closely with the director to create the final cut of the film.
7. **Sound Designer:** The sound designer is responsible for creating the sound effects and music for the film. They work closely with the director to create the desired mood and atmosphere.
8. **Actors:** Actors are responsible for bringing the characters in the script to life. They work closely with the director to

create the desired performances and bring their characters to life on screen.
9. Production Manager: The production manager is responsible for overseeing the day-to-day operations of the production. They work closely with the producer to
10. ensure that everything runs smoothly and on schedule.

These are just a few of the many different roles involved in film production, and each person has their own unique responsibilities. By working together, these individuals create a cohesive and engaging film that can captivate audiences and inspire emotions.

Storytelling

What is a synopsis versus a treatment

In the world of film, a synopsis and a treatment are both important tools for filmmakers to create a clear and compelling narrative for their movies.

A synopsis is a brief summary of the story, usually around one or two pages in length. It provides an overview of the plot, main characters, and key events in the story. A synopsis is used by producers, executives, and agents to quickly understand the main idea of a movie and decide whether or not to invest in it.

A treatment, on the other hand, is a more detailed document that outlines the story and characters in greater depth, often spanning several pages. It is used by writers, directors, and producers to flesh out the story and explore the characters' motivations and emotions. A treatment is often used as a blueprint for the scriptwriting process and may include scene descriptions, dialogue, and even visual ideas.

Here are some guidelines for creating a synopsis for a film:

Start with a clear logline: The logline should be a brief sentence that summarizes the story and captures the attention of the reader.

Focus on the main plot: The synopsis should focus on the main plot and avoid getting bogged down in details.

Include the main characters: The synopsis should include the main characters and their roles in the story.

Emphasize the conflict: The synopsis should highlight the central conflict of the story, including the obstacles that the characters must overcome.

Keep it concise: The synopsis should be one or two pages in length and should avoid unnecessary details or subplots.

Use present tense: Write the synopsis in the present tense to give the reader a sense of immediacy and engagement.

End with a strong hook: The synopsis should end with a strong hook that leaves the reader wanting to know more.

When writing a synopsis, it's important to remember that it's not a detailed outline of the story. Instead, it's a brief summary that captures the essence of the story and makes the reader want to learn more. By following these guidelines, filmmakers can create a compelling synopsis that showcases the best aspects of their story and helps attract potential investors or collaborators.

What Is Visual Storytelling?

Visual storytelling is a way of telling a story using pictures or videos to convey emotions, messages, or ideas. It is a powerful tool that helps people connect with the story on a deeper level and makes it easier to understand and remember.

Think of it this way: when you watch a movie, you're not just watching actors reciting lines. You're seeing the characters' facial expressions, their body language, and the world they inhabit. You're hearing the music, sound effects, and dialogue. All of these elements work together to create a story that engages your senses and emotions.

Visual storytelling is similar in that it uses images and other visual elements to tell a story. This can include things like photographs, illustrations, infographics, and videos. By using visuals, the storyteller can create a more immersive experience that captures the viewer's attention and makes them feel like they are part of the story.

For example, imagine you're reading a book about a character who is lost in the woods. The author might describe the character's fear and confusion, but it can be difficult to really imagine what that would look like. However, if you see an illustration of the character stumbling through a dark forest, it becomes easier to empathize with their situation and understand what they are going through.

Visual storytelling is especially important in today's world, where we are bombarded with information from all sides. By using compelling visuals, storytellers can cut through the noise and capture their audience's attention. This is why you see so many videos, infographics, and other visual content online - it's an effective way to communicate a message in a way that people will remember.

So, whether you're watching a movie, reading a comic book, or scrolling through Instagram, you're experiencing visual storytelling. It's a powerful way to tell a story, and it can be a lot of fun to explore all the different ways that people use visuals to convey their ideas and emotions.

STORYTELLING SCRIPTS

Where do idea for movie scripts comes from and how do you create interest for conflicts for your characters

Creating conflict and resolution is a crucial aspect of storytelling in film, as it keeps the audience engaged and invested in the characters and their journey. Here are some techniques to create conflict and resolution in a film:

Character-driven conflict: Conflict can arise from the differences between characters' goals, motivations, and values. For example, in a romantic film, the conflict might arise from the differences in the characters' lifestyles, personalities, or social status.

External conflict: Conflict can also arise from external factors, such as a natural disaster, a war, or a criminal threat. For example, in an action movie, the conflict might arise from the protagonist's mission to stop a terrorist attack or save hostages.

Internal conflict: Conflict can also arise from a character's internal struggles, such as a moral dilemma, guilt, or fear. For example, in a drama film, the conflict might arise from a character's decision to confront a difficult truth about themselves or others.

Plot-driven conflict: Conflict can also arise from the plot's events and twists, such as a sudden betrayal, a plot twist, or a surprise revelation. For example, in a thriller film, the conflict might arise from the protagonist's attempts to unravel a conspiracy or a secret plot.

To create a resolution, the conflict must be resolved in a way that satisfies the audience and brings closure to the story. Here are some techniques for creating resolution:

Character growth: The resolution can show how the character has grown and changed as a result of the conflict. For example, in a coming-of-age film, the resolution might show how the protagonist has matured and learned important life lessons.

Compromise: The resolution can show how the characters have found a compromise or common ground to resolve their differences. For example, in a romantic film, the resolution might show how the couple has found a way to bridge their differences and build a happy relationship.

Redemption: The resolution can show how the characters have redeemed themselves after a mistake or wrongdoing. For example, in a drama film, the resolution might show how the character has made amends for their past actions and found inner peace.

Adaptation is the process of creating a film script based on pre-existing material, such as real-life events, news stories, historical events, magazine articles, or even dreams and fantasy situations. Here are some techniques for adapting a story into a film script:

Focus on the central conflict: Identify the central conflict of the story and focus on it when adapting it into a film script. This will help you streamline the story and create a cohesive narrative that works well on screen.

Visualize the story: When adapting a story, it's essential to visualize how it will look on screen. Consider how you can use visuals, sound, and dialogue to bring the story to life and make it engaging for the audience.

Make changes to the story: When adapting a story, it's often necessary to make changes to make it work better as a film. This can include altering the timeline, combining or eliminating characters, and changing the ending.

Be true to the source material: While changes may be necessary, it's important to stay true to the core of the story and its themes. This will ensure that the adaptation resonates with the original material's fans while also appealing to a broader audience.

In summary, conflict and resolution are essential storytelling techniques in film, while adaptation is the process of creating a film script based on pre-existing material. By using these techniques effectively, filmmakers can create compelling and engaging stories that resonate with their audiences.

How to write a script for different genres of movies

Writing a movie script can be a daunting task, but with some structure and guidelines, you can create a compelling story for any genre of movie. Here are some tips for writing and structuring movie scripts for different genres:

1. **Action Movie:**
   - Start with a high-stakes conflict that sets the tone for the rest of the movie
   - Introduce the main character as a capable and charismatic hero or heroine
   - Create a clear and consistent villain with a personal connection to the hero
   - Build tension through action sequences that escalate in intensity throughout the movie
   - Provide a satisfying resolution that rewards the hero's bravery and skill

2. **Romantic Movie:**
   - Establish the setting and tone to create a romantic atmosphere
   - Create compelling characters with distinct personalities, desires, and obstacles to overcome
   - Develop a believable and emotionally charged romantic relationship between the main characters
   - Use dialogue, gestures, and small moments to show the depth of the characters' feelings for each other
   - Resolve the conflicts that keep the couple apart in a way that is both satisfying and true to the story

3. **Comedy Movie:**
   - Establish the comedic tone and style of the movie from the beginning
   - Create larger-than-life characters with exaggerated personalities and quirks

- Develop a plot that relies on misunderstandings, mistaken identity, and other comedic tropes
- Use witty dialogue and physical comedy to generate laughs
- Provide a satisfying and unexpected ending that resolves the conflicts and reinforces the movie's comedic themes

4. Drama Movie:
- Establish a clear and emotionally resonant conflict that drives the story
- Create complex characters with realistic flaws and motivations
- Develop a plot that explores the characters' relationships, values, and struggles
- Use dialogue and visuals to convey the depth of the characters' emotions
- Provide a resolution that is both surprising and true to the characters' journeys

5. Thriller Movie:
- Create a sense of tension and suspense from the beginning of the movie
- Introduce the main character as an underdog or outsider who is up against a powerful and mysterious villain
- Develop a plot that involves twists and turns, betrayals, and unexpected revelations
- Use visual and audio cues to build suspense and keep the audience on the edge of their seats
- Provide a resolution that satisfies the audience's desire for justice and closure

6. Science Fiction Movie:
- Establish the setting and rules of the sci-fi world

- Create complex and believable characters with clear motivations and desires
- Develop a plot that explores the implications of the sci-fi world on the characters and the story
- Use futuristic technology, settings, and themes to create a sense of awe and wonder
- Provide a satisfying resolution that uses sci-fi elements to drive the story and reinforce the themes of the movie

In general, the key to writing a successful movie script is to create a compelling story with memorable characters, clear conflicts, and a satisfying resolution. Each genre has its own unique requirements and conventions, but by following these guidelines and structuring your script appropriately, you can create a movie that resonates with your audience and stands the test of time

Archetypes

In visual storytelling and film, archetypes refer to universal characters, symbols, and themes that are deeply ingrained in human consciousness and have been passed down through generations of storytelling. These archetypes represent fundamental human experiences, emotions, and desires, and they serve as shorthand for audiences to quickly understand and connect with the characters and the story.

Some common archetypes in visual storytelling and film include the hero, the villain, the mentor, the trickster, the lover, the explorer, and the innocent. Each archetype has a distinct set of characteristics, motivations, and goals that resonate with audiences on a subconscious level. For example, the hero archetype is typically depicted as brave, noble, and willing to sacrifice themselves for the greater good, while the villain archetype is often characterized as cunning, manipulative, and ruthless.

Using archetypes in visual storytelling and film can help create compelling characters and stories that resonate with audiences. By drawing on these universal symbols and themes, filmmakers can tap into the collective human experience and create stories that are emotionally resonant and powerful.

Be the hero

The Hero's Journey is a storytelling structure that was first identified and popularized by the American scholar and mythologist Joseph Campbell in his book "The Hero with a Thousand Faces." It describes a common pattern that appears in many myths, legends, and stories from around the world. This pattern involves a hero who embarks on a journey, faces challenges and obstacles, and ultimately achieves some kind of transformation or victory.

The Hero's Journey typically involves several stages, including the call to adventure, the refusal of the call, the crossing of the threshold into the unknown, the encounter with allies and enemies, the ordeal or crisis, the reward or transformation, and the return home. Along the way, the hero may encounter various archetypes, such as the mentor, the trickster, and the shadow.

Campbell argued that this pattern is not just a feature of ancient myths and legends, but can be found in many modern stories as well. He suggested that this is because the Hero's Journey reflects something deep and universal about human experience, particularly the human desire to seek meaning and purpose in life.

The influence of the Hero's Journey can be seen in many modern storytelling forms, including books, films, and television shows. For example, George Lucas has acknowledged that he was influenced by Campbell's ideas when creating the Star Wars franchise. The journey of Luke Skywalker from humble farm boy to Jedi Knight follows many of the stages of the Hero's Journey. Other examples of modern-day heroes who follow the Hero's Journey include Harry Potter, Katniss Everdeen, and Neo from The Matrix.

Character and character viewpoint and development

When writing a character's viewpoint, it is important to consider their background, beliefs, and values. This will help to create a unique perspective for the character and add depth to their portrayal. Additionally, it is important to consider how the character's viewpoint may change throughout the course of the story as they experience different events and interactions with other characters.

The hero's journey by Joseph Campbell is a popular storytelling structure that can be applied to many different types of stories, including movies. This structure typically involves a hero who goes on a journey of self-discovery and faces various challenges and obstacles along the way before ultimately achieving their goal.

To increase a character's presence in a film, it can be helpful to give them distinct personality traits and mannerisms that make them stand out. Additionally, the character should have clear motivations and goals that drive their actions throughout the story. It is also important to ensure that the character's actions and decisions are consistent with their personality and background. By developing well-rounded and believable characters, the audience will be more invested in the story and the characters' journeys.

Lesson Title: Archetypes in Film: How to Create a Memorable Character

Objective: Students will be able to identify and create archetypes in films and understand their origins in Greek mythology and fables.

Materials Needed:

- Whiteboard or chalkboard
- Writing utensils
- Film clips or movie examples

Introduction (10 minutes):

- Ask students if they have ever heard of the term "archetype" and what it means to them.
- Explain that archetypes are universal symbols or patterns that have been present in storytelling for thousands of years.
- Discuss the origins of archetypes in Greek mythology and fables.

Body (30 minutes):

- Introduce several common archetypes in films such as the Hero, the Villain, the Mentor, the Trickster, and the Innocent.
- Show examples of these archetypes in popular films and have students identify which archetype the character represents.
- Have students work in pairs or groups to create their own character based on an archetype. They should consider the character's personality traits, strengths, weaknesses, and motivations.
- Encourage students to use their imagination and be creative with their characters.
- After the activity, have each group share their character with the class and explain which archetype they used as inspiration.

Conclusion (10 minutes):

- Recap the concept of archetypes and how they are used in storytelling.
- Discuss the importance of creating memorable characters that the audience can connect with.
- Encourage students to think about how they can incorporate archetypes in their own storytelling.

Assessment:

- Students will be assessed on their participation in the group activity and their ability to identify and explain an archetype in a film.

How to create a character for a when you are making a movie

When creating a film, creating a compelling character and a well-crafted plot are two essential elements to making a successful movie. Here are some tips on how to create a character and a plot for a film:

Creating a Character:

Know your character's backstory: Understanding a character's history can help you create a more well-rounded and believable character. What was their childhood like? What major events have shaped who they are today?

Identify your character's strengths and weaknesses: Characters should have unique personalities that make them stand out from the other characters. Knowing your character's strengths and weaknesses will help you understand how they will react to certain situations in the film.

Give your character a goal: Your character needs a clear objective to work towards throughout the film. This goal should be challenging, and the character should face obstacles along the way that will help them grow and change.

Create a physical appearance: The physical appearance of a character is an essential aspect of their identity. Consider how the character's clothing, hair, and makeup can communicate their personality, occupation, and mood.

Lesson Plan: The Hero's Journey in Modern Storytelling

Grade Level: High School

Objective: Students will understand the concept of The Hero's Journey by Joseph Campbell and its influence on modern storytelling. They will be able to identify the stages of The Hero's Journey in a modern-day hero.

Materials:

- Copies of the book "The Hero with a Thousand Faces" by Joseph Campbell
- Handout with The Hero's Journey stages
- Video examples of modern-day heroes (e.g. Harry Potter, Katniss Everdeen, Luke Skywalker)

Introduction (15 minutes):

- Introduce The Hero's Journey concept and Joseph Campbell's book "The Hero with a Thousand Faces"
- Show examples of modern-day heroes in movies and books
- Discuss how these characters fit into The Hero's Journey structure
- Hand out The Hero's Journey stages handout

Activity 1 (25 minutes):

- Have students watch a video example of a modern-day hero (e.g. Harry Potter, Katniss Everdeen, Luke Skywalker)
- Have them identify the stages of The Hero's Journey in the character's story
- Discuss as a class and write down the identified stages on the board

Activity 2 (25 minutes):

- Divide students into groups
- Have them choose a modern-day hero and create a presentation identifying the stages of The Hero's Journey in the character's story
- Encourage creativity and engagement through visual aids, sound effects, or role-playing
- Each group will present their findings to the class

Closure (15 minutes):

- Recap the stages of The Hero's Journey as a class

- Discuss the importance of The Hero's Journey in modern storytelling and how it affects our understanding of characters and their journeys

Assessment:

- Students will be assessed on their participation in class discussions, ability to identify The Hero's Journey stages in a modern-day hero's story, and the creativity and effectiveness of their group presentations.

Example of a Modern-Day Hero:

Title: Black Panther Character: T'Challa/Black Panther

11. The Ordinary World: T'Challa lives in the technologically advanced African nation of Wakanda, where he is next in line to become king.
12. The Call to Adventure: After his father's death, T'Challa must take on the role of king and become the Black Panther.
13. Refusal of the Call: T'Challa initially struggles with the responsibility of leading his nation and wearing the mantle of the Black Panther.
14. Meeting the Mentor: T'Challa seeks guidance from his mother, his sister, and the spiritual leader of Wakanda.
15. Crossing the Threshold: T'Challa leaves Wakanda to retrieve stolen vibranium, which leads him to encounter Erik Killmonger.
16. Tests, Allies, Enemies: T'Challa is aided by his loyal friend and ally, Okoye, as he faces Killmonger and his allies.
17. Approach to the Inmost Cave: T'Challa confronts Killmonger and learns the truth about his family and Wakanda's past.
18. Ordeal: T'Challa loses his powers and is presumed dead by his allies and enemies.
19. Reward: T'Challa is revived by his mother and his allies and regains his powers.

20. The Road Back: T'Challa returns to Wakanda and prepares to face Killmonger in a final battle.
21. Resurrection: T'Challa and Killmonger engage in a battle for the throne and Wakanda's future.
22. Return with the Elixir: T'Challa emerges victorious and brings Wakanda into a new era of openness and leadership.

CHARACTER DEVELOPMENT

Characters and environments are both essential elements of any film as they help to establish the story, create emotional connections with the audience, and provide context for the events taking place on screen.

Characters serve as the driving force of the story, allowing the audience to connect with and empathize with their struggles and experiences. A well-developed character can provide a sense of relatability, creating a deeper emotional investment in the story. The environment, on the other hand, serves as a backdrop for the characters and their actions, providing context and atmosphere to the story. A well-crafted environment can help to immerse the audience in the world of the film, making the story feel more real and impactful.

Cinema verité is a filmmaking technique that emerged in the 1960s, emphasizing the use of naturalistic and observational methods to capture real-life events and experiences. This technique often involves filming real people and events without scripted dialogue or formal structure, creating a sense of authenticity and realism. An example of cinema verité is the 1963 documentary "Primary," which follows the campaign of John F. Kennedy and Hubert Humphrey during the 1960 Wisconsin Democratic presidential primary.

Juxtaposition is a technique that involves placing two or more contrasting elements together in order to create a new meaning or perspective. This technique can be used to highlight the differences or similarities between characters, environments, or ideas. Juxtaposition has been used in cinema since its early days, with examples like D.W. Griffith's 1915 film "The Birth of a Nation" which used contrasting shots of peaceful plantation life and chaotic battle scenes to make a political point. In contemporary cinema, juxtaposition can be seen in films like "Moonlight" (2016), which contrasts the different stages of a character's life to explore themes of identity and self-discovery.

In conclusion, characters and environments are important elements in creating a compelling film. They help to establish the story, create emotional connections with the audience, and provide context for the events taking place on screen. Techniques like cinema verité and juxtaposition can be used to add depth and meaning to these elements, helping to create a more impactful and memorable film.

Creating a Plot:

Identify your film's genre: The genre of your film will help dictate the type of story you want to tell. For example, a romantic comedy will have a different plot than an action film.

Create a central conflict: The conflict is the main problem that the protagonist must overcome to achieve their goal. The conflict should be clear, and the audience should understand what is at stake if the character fails.

Develop a story structure: A well-structured story has a clear beginning, middle, and end. Consider how your story will unfold and what pivotal moments will occur throughout the film.

Introduce subplots: Subplots can add depth and complexity to your story. Consider introducing secondary characters or storylines that will intersect with the main plot and provide additional challenges for the protagonist.

Create a satisfying resolution: The ending of your film should be satisfying and provide closure for the audience. The resolution should tie up any loose ends and provide a sense of catharsis.

In conclusion, creating a character and plot for a film requires careful planning and attention to detail. By taking the time to develop a well-rounded character and a compelling story, you can create a movie that resonates with your audience and leaves a lasting impact.

FORMAT FOR A ANY MOVIE SCRIPT

TITLE: The Great Adventure

SUBTITLE: A Tale of Love and Treasure

WRITTEN BY: John Smith

COPYRIGHT: ©2023 John Smith

CAST:

    Jack - male, 30s, ruggedly handsome

    Lily - female, 20s, spirited and adventurous

    Captain Black - male, 50s, grizzled and menacing

    Crew Members - various male and female, 20s-40s

CHARACTERS:

    Jack

    Lily

    Captain Black

    Crew Members

MARGINS: 1 inch on all sides

NUMBERING: Each page is numbered in the top right corner

SLUGLINE: INT/EXT, Location, Day/Night

TRANSITIONS: FADE IN, CUT TO, DISSOLVE TO, FADE OUT

ANGLES: WIDE SHOT, MEDIUM SHOT, CLOSE-UP, EXTREME CLOSE-UP, OVER-THE-SHOULDER, BIRD'S EYE VIEW, LOW ANGLE, HIGH ANGLE

ACTS: Typically a script is divided into three acts

LENGTH: Approximately 90-120 pages for a feature-length film

SYNTAX: Present tense, active voice

GRAMMAR: Use proper punctuation and capitalization

INT. JUNGLE - DAY

Jack and Lily hack their way through the dense foliage. They're both sweaty and tired.

JACK

(whispers)

We're getting close. I can feel it.

LILY

(whispers)

What do you think we'll find?

JACK

(smiling)

Treasure. Lots and lots of treasure.

Suddenly, they hear a rustling in the bushes. They both draw their swords.

CUT TO:

EXT. BEACH - DAY

Jack and Lily emerge from the jungle onto a beautiful beach. The sun is shining and the waves are crashing against the shore.

ANGLE ON: Captain Black and his crew standing in front of a large pirate ship.

CAPTAIN BLACK

(smiling)

Welcome to your doom, Jack.

Jack and Lily draw their swords and charge towards the pirates.

FADE OUT.

THE END.

In this example, the title of the film is "The Great Adventure" and it is a tale

STORYTELLING

"TIMELESS LOVERS" EXAMPLE OF A SYNPOSIS

young talented street artist from Italy by the name of Joseph who works in times square and paints tourist portraits for a living meets a beautiful young woman by the name of Annabella from California whose wealthy family hates the fact that she has falls in love with the young artist by the name of Joseph

Joseph is a young and talented street artist from Italy who works in Times Square, New York City. He earns his living by painting portraits of tourists, impressing them with his artistic skills and creativity. Despite the challenges he faces as a street artist, Joseph is determined to pursue his passion for art and make a name for himself in the world of painting.

One day, Joseph meets a beautiful young woman named Annabella, who is visiting from California. Annabella is instantly drawn to Joseph's work and struck by his charming personality. As they spend more time together, they realize they have a strong connection and fall deeply in love.

However, Annabella's wealthy family is strongly against their relationship, as they do not approve of her being a street artist. They pressure Annabella to end the relationship, threatening to cut her off from the family's wealth and status if she continues to see Joseph.

Despite the challenges they face, Joseph and Annabella are determined to stay together and fight for their love. Joseph continues to paint and showcase his talent, hoping to one day make a breakthrough in the art world. Annabella supports him in his endeavors, even if it means going against her family's wishes.

Together, they navigate the obstacles in their path and strive to build a life together, proving that love knows no bounds and that art has the power to bring people together.

STORYTELLING

Example of Dialogue for a film

Joseph: painting a portrait of Annabella "You know, Annabella, I've painted countless portraits of tourists here in Times Square, but there's something special about you. Your beauty is truly captivating."

Annabella: blushing "Thank you, Joseph. You're quite the charmer yourself."

Joseph: "I'm just being honest. I see so much beauty in the world around me, and I try to capture it in my paintings. That's why I love being a street artist."

Annabella: "I can see that. Your passion for art is truly inspiring."

Joseph: "And you inspire me, Annabella. I feel like I can be myself around you, like I don't have to hide my true self."

Annabella: "I feel the same way. But my family, they don't understand us. They think that because you're a street artist, you're not good enough for me."

Joseph: "Don't listen to them, Annabella. We have something real, something special. We can make it work, despite what anyone else says."

Annabella: "I believe that too. I'll do whatever it takes to be with you, Joseph."

Joseph: "Then let's prove them wrong. Let's show them that love knows no boundaries, and that art has the power to bring people together."

STORYTELLING

Example of a Shooting Script

ANNABELLA

(passionately)

He's not just some street artist. He's Joseph. And he's everything to me.

CUT TO:

EXT. TIMES SQUARE - DAY

Joseph is painting a portrait of Annabella when Mr. and Mrs. Winters show up.

MR. WINTERS

(angrily)

Joseph, is it? We need to have a talk.

Joseph tries to defend himself, but Mr. Winters is having none of it.

CUT TO:

INT. ANNABELLA'S BEDROOM - DAY

Annabella is packing her bags.

MRS. WINTERS

(disapprovingly)

You're going away with him? What about your family? Your future?

ANNABELLA

(passionately)

I love him, Mom. And I won't let anyone come between us.

CUT TO:

EXT. TIMES SQUARE - NIGHT

Annabella and Joseph meet up in Times Square, ready to start their new life together.

ANNABELLA

(happily)

I don't care what anyone says. As long as I'm with you, that's all that matters.

JOSEPH

(smiling)

That's all that matters to me too.

They share a kiss as the camera pans up to the Times Square lights.

FADE TO BLACK.

Lesson Plan: Visual Storytelling for Teens

Objective:

To teach teens how to effectively use visual elements to tell a story through the creation of a short film.

Materials:

Cameras or smartphones

Computer with video editing software (e.g. iMovie, Adobe Premiere)

Access to sound effects and music libraries

Storyboard templates

Paper and pencils

Introduction (15 mins):

Start by asking students what they think makes a good story. Encourage them to consider both written and visual storytelling.

Introduce the concept of visual storytelling and explain that it is the art of communicating a story through images and sequences. Provide examples of visual storytelling such as movies, television shows, and comic books.

Discuss the importance of planning and organization in visual storytelling by showing them storyboard templates and explaining how they can help structure a story.

Activity 1: Storyboarding (30 mins)

Divide students into groups of 3-4.

Provide each group with a storyboard template and ask them to brainstorm a short story that they would like to tell through a film.

Encourage them to consider elements such as setting, characters, and conflict. They should also think about how they can use camera angles, lighting, and other visual techniques to enhance their story.

Have each group present their storyboard to the class, explaining their story and how they plan to visually communicate it.

Activity 2: Filming (60 mins)

Once each group has a finalized storyboard, give them access to cameras or smartphones and have them film their story.

Encourage them to experiment with different camera angles, lighting, and other visual techniques to bring their story to life.

Remind them to focus on the storytelling aspect, rather than just creating visually stunning shots.

As they film, remind them to keep in mind the elements they discussed in their storyboard.

Activity 3: Editing (45 mins)

After filming is complete, have students transfer their footage to a computer and begin editing.

Provide a brief tutorial on using video editing software and show them how to import their footage, arrange clips, and add transitions.

Encourage them to experiment with different sound effects and music to enhance their story.

Remind them to focus on pacing and sequencing to effectively communicate their story.

Conclusion (10 mins)

Once students have completed their films, have them present their finished products to the class.

Encourage them to provide feedback to each other and discuss what worked well and what could be improved.

Recap the importance of planning and organization in visual storytelling, as well as the role of camera angles, lighting, and sound in effectively communicating a story.

STORYTELLING

PROTAGONIST AND AN ANTOGNIST

The protagonist and antagonist are two of the most important characters in a movie script. The protagonist is the main character, who is usually the hero of the story and is on a mission to achieve a goal. On the other hand, the antagonist is the character who opposes the protagonist and creates conflict in the story. The antagonist is often portrayed as the villain or the person who stands in the way of the protagonist's goals.

To help explain the difference between the two to 9-12 graders, we can use the example of the movie Titanic. In this movie, the protagonist is Jack, who is portrayed as the hero of the story. He is a poor artist who wins a ticket to board the Titanic and falls in love with Rose, the daughter of a wealthy businessman. Jack's goal is to win Rose's heart and start a new life with her.

The antagonist, in this case, is Rose's fiancé, Cal. He is the character who opposes Jack and creates conflict in the story. Cal is portrayed as a wealthy and entitled man who wants to marry Rose for her family's money and status. Cal's goal is to keep Rose away from Jack and maintain his position of power.

To help students understand how other characters in the movie should relate to the protagonist and antagonist, we can create a lesson plan that involves analyzing the relationships between the characters. Here are some possible activities:

Character Analysis: Have students analyze the personalities, motivations, and actions of the protagonist and antagonist. Ask them to describe how they perceive each character and why they think the characters act the way they do.

Role-playing: Divide students into groups and assign each group a character from the movie. Have them act out scenes from the movie or create their own scenes where they interact with other characters. Encourage them to stay in character and think about how their character would react to other characters.

Group Discussion: Have a class discussion about the relationships between the characters in the movie. Ask students to identify the conflicts and how they are resolved. Encourage them to think about how the protagonist and antagonist affect the other characters and how they influence the plot.

By understanding the roles of the protagonist and antagonist in a movie, and how other characters relate to them, students can gain a better understanding of the story and how it unfolds.

Lesson Plan : Teens and Young Adults Who want to become a Film Director

Title: Learning to Become a Movie Director

Grade Level: Teenagers and adults

Objective:

Students will learn about the basic concepts and techniques involved in directing a film and will create their own short film.

Materials:

Whiteboard and markers

Handouts with information on directing techniques

Camera or smartphone

Editing software (optional)

Lesson Plan:

Introduction:

Begin by asking students if they have ever thought about making a movie or if they have any favorite films or directors. Discuss the role of a movie director and how they contribute to the creative vision of a film.

Directing Techniques:

Introduce students to the basic concepts and techniques involved in directing a film. Cover topics such as camera angles, shot composition, lighting, and sound. Use handouts or visual aids to help students understand these concepts.

Scene Analysis:

Divide students into small groups and provide them with a short film clip to analyze. Ask them to identify the techniques used in the scene, such as camera angles, lighting, and sound. Discuss how these techniques contribute to the mood and tone of the scene.

Storyboarding:

Introduce students to the concept of storyboarding, which is a visual representation of a film's scenes and shots. Provide them with a blank storyboard template and ask them to create a storyboard for a short scene.

Filming:

Provide students with a camera or smartphone and ask them to film their own short scene. Encourage them to experiment with different camera angles and techniques.

Editing:

If possible, provide students with editing software and ask them to edit their film. Discuss the importance of editing in creating a cohesive and engaging film.

Screening:

Finally, screen the students' films and discuss what they learned from the experience. Encourage them to share their thoughts on the process of directing a film and how it influenced their filmmaking decisions.

Conclusion:

Wrap up the lesson by discussing the importance of collaboration in filmmaking and how different roles on a film set work together to create a final product. Encourage students to continue exploring their creativity and to pursue their interests in filmmaking.

DIRECTING

Techniques to consider for effective movie directing

Directing a movie is a complex and multi-faceted task that involves a wide range of techniques and skills. Here are some of the key directing techniques that can help students learn how to direct a movie effectively:

Camera Placement and Movement: The placement and movement of the camera are critical in setting the tone and mood of a scene. Directors need to decide on the camera placement and movement that best conveys the emotional and narrative aspects of a scene. For example, a static shot can create a sense of stability, while a moving camera can generate tension or excitement.

Framing and Composition: Directors must also consider how to frame the shot, including what elements will be included in the frame, and how they will be arranged. This includes decisions about the use of foreground, midground, and background elements, as well as the rule of thirds, which involves dividing the frame into thirds both horizontally and vertically.

Lighting: The use of lighting is essential to set the mood and tone of a scene. Directors must make decisions about the quality, direction, and color of the light. They must also decide which areas of the frame will be illuminated or shadowed.

Sound: The use of sound can dramatically impact the emotional impact of a scene. Directors need to decide on the volume, clarity, and type of sound that will be used. This includes dialogue, music, sound effects, and ambient noise.

Blocking and Movement: Blocking involves the movement and positioning of actors within the frame. Directors must make decisions about how to direct the actors in terms of their movements and expressions, as well as their interactions with other actors and objects within the scene.

Pace and Rhythm: The pace and rhythm of a scene can be used to build tension, suspense, or excitement. Directors must make decisions about the timing and duration of shots, as well as the use of editing techniques such as cuts, dissolves, and fades.

Genre-Specific Techniques: Finally, directors must be familiar with genre-specific techniques that can be used to effectively convey the genre of the film. For example, horror films often make use of jump scares and suspenseful music, while action films may use fast-paced editing and a variety of camera angles to convey movement and excitement.

In conclusion, learning the different directing techniques is essential for students who want to learn how to direct a movie effectively. By mastering these techniques, directors can create compelling and emotionally impactful films that resonate with audiences.

DIRECTING UNDERSTANDING CAMERA ANGLES

Students Learning Film Directing

Welcome to the world of film directing! As a director, your job is to visually tell a story using a variety of camera angles, shots, and techniques. In this manual, we will go over some of the essential camera angles and shots, along with their purposes and the moods they can convey to the audience.

Camera Angles

Eye Level Shot - This angle is the most common and straightforward angle used in films. It is shot from a level camera angle that matches the height of the character. It is neutral and does not convey any specific mood.

High Angle Shot - This angle is shot from above the character and can make the character appear vulnerable, weak, or powerless.

Low Angle Shot - This angle is shot from below the character and can make the character appear dominant, powerful, or heroic.

Dutch Angle Shot - This angle is shot with a tilted camera that creates an unbalanced or disorienting effect. It can be used to convey a sense of unease, tension, or instability.

God Angle Shot - This angle is shot from an extremely high angle, looking down on the character, and can be used to emphasize the character's insignificance or vulnerability.

Camera Shots

Wide Shot - This shot shows the entire scene or setting and is used to establish location and context. It can also be used to convey a sense of isolation or vulnerability.

Medium Shot - This shot shows the character from the waist up and is used to establish the character's physical presence and body language. It can also be used to convey a sense of intimacy or connection.

Close-up Shot - This shot shows the character's face and is used to convey emotion or intensity. It can also be used to create a sense of intimacy or tension.

Extreme Close-up Shot - This shot shows a very small detail of the character, such as their eyes or mouth. It is used to convey extreme emotion or intensity.

Medium Close-up Shot - This shot shows the character from the chest up and is used to establish the character's emotions and reactions. It can also be used to convey a sense of intimacy or connection.

Mood

Wide Shot - Conveys a sense of space, isolation, or vulnerability.

Medium Shot - Conveys a sense of intimacy, connection, or physical presence.

Close-up Shot - Conveys emotion, intensity, or tension.

Extreme Close-up Shot - Conveys extreme emotion or intensity.

Medium Close-up Shot - Conveys emotion, reactions, or intimacy.

In conclusion, mastering the use of camera angles and shots is essential for film directors who want to create compelling and emotionally impactful films. By understanding the purposes and moods conveyed by each angle and shot, directors can effectively tell their stories and captivate their audiences.

DIRECTING

How to create mood and tone when making a movie

Creating the right mood and tone is essential for filmmakers to effectively convey the story and emotions to their audience. Here are some tips on how to create the desired mood and tone when filming a movie:

Choose the right location: The location plays a vital role in setting the mood and tone for a scene. The right location can evoke the desired emotions and enhance the story's atmosphere. For instance, a dark alley can create a sense of danger or foreboding, while a bright, sunny park can create a sense of joy and happiness.

Use lighting to your advantage: Lighting can significantly affect the mood and tone of a scene. By manipulating light sources and creating shadows, you can create a sense of mystery, tension, or drama. For example, using low-key lighting, with most of the scene in shadow, can create a moody and suspenseful atmosphere.

Select the right colors: Colors can have a significant impact on the mood of a scene. For instance, red can evoke feelings of passion, danger, or anger, while blue can create a sense of calmness, sadness, or melancholy. Using color contrasts and saturation levels can also influence the tone of the scene.

Use music and sound effects: Music and sound effects can help set the tone for a scene and create the desired mood. For instance, a suspenseful soundtrack can create a sense of tension, while soft, calming music can create a peaceful or romantic atmosphere. Sound effects can also be used to heighten the mood and add realism to the scene.

Consider the camera angles and movement: Camera angles and movement can significantly affect the mood and tone of a scene. For example, using low angles can make the characters appear more dominant, while high angles can make them appear vulnerable or weak. Camera movement, such as tracking shots or shaky handheld shots, can also create a sense of tension, urgency, or chaos.

Use pacing and editing: The pacing and editing of a scene can also influence the mood and tone. Slow, deliberate pacing can create a sense of suspense or anticipation, while fast-paced editing can create a sense of excitement or urgency.

In conclusion, creating the desired mood and tone when filming a movie requires careful consideration of various factors, including location, lighting, colors, music, sound effects, camera angles, movement, pacing, and editing. By using these tools effectively, filmmakers can effectively convey their story and emotions to the audience, creating a powerful and impactful cinematic experience.

DIRECTING

What is Framing and compositing

Framing and composition refer to the visual elements that filmmakers use to create a specific look and feel in their movies. It involves placing and arranging subjects, objects, and the camera in a way that conveys a particular message or emotion to the audience.

Here are some framing and composition techniques commonly used in filmmaking:

Rule of thirds: The rule of thirds is a fundamental composition technique used in both photography and filmmaking. It involves dividing the frame into three sections horizontally and vertically, creating a grid of nine equal squares. By placing the main subject at one of the intersecting points, the composition becomes more balanced and visually appealing. For example, in the movie "The Shawshank Redemption," the shot of the protagonist, Andy, sitting on a rock at the end of a sewage tunnel is framed using the rule of thirds, with Andy positioned at the intersection of two lines.

Centered composition: Centered composition involves placing the main subject directly in the center of the frame. This technique can create a sense of stability and balance. For example, in the movie "The Godfather," the shot of Don Corleone sitting in his chair during his daughter's wedding is centered, emphasizing his importance and power.

Close-ups: Close-up shots focus on a specific object or subject, emphasizing its importance or emotional significance. For example, in the movie "Gone with the Wind," the close-up shot of Scarlett O'Hara's face as she declares that she will never go hungry again conveys her determination and resilience.

Wide shots: Wide shots show the entire scene, providing context and setting. For example, in the movie "Jurassic Park," the wide shot of the T-Rex enclosure shows the vastness and danger of the dinosaur world.

Depth of field: Depth of field refers to the range of focus in a shot, from the foreground to the background. By adjusting the aperture and focus, filmmakers can control the depth of field and draw attention to specific areas of the frame. For example, in the movie "The Revenant," the shallow depth of field in the shot of Hugh Glass crawling out of his grave emphasizes his isolation and vulnerability.

Dutch angle: The Dutch angle is a technique that tilts the camera to create an unbalanced and disorienting effect. This technique is often used in thrillers or horror movies to create a sense of tension and unease. For example, in the movie "The Dark Knight," the Dutch angle shot of the Joker hanging upside down adds to his unpredictability and instability.

In conclusion, framing and composition are essential techniques that filmmakers use to create specific visual effects and convey emotions and messages to their audience. By carefully selecting and arranging the visual elements, filmmakers can create a powerful and impactful cinematic experience.

DIRECTING

Lesson Plan: Understanding Pace and Rhythm in Filmmaking

Objective: To teach students about the importance of pace and rhythm in filmmaking and how it affects the audience's emotional response to the film.

Target Audience: Students aged 11-21 years old interested in filmmaking, specifically in the genres of action, romantic, thriller, suspense, horror, or sci-fi movies.

Materials:

Examples of films from the aforementioned genres

Whiteboard or chalkboard

Markers or chalk

Handouts with definitions and examples

Introduction:

Ask students if they've ever watched a movie that felt too slow or too fast-paced.

Discuss how the pace and rhythm of a film can affect the audience's emotions and engagement with the story.

Explain that in this lesson, they will learn about the different techniques filmmakers use to control the pace and rhythm of a film.

Body:

Define Pace and Rhythm

Write the definitions on the board and discuss them with the class.

Pace: the speed at which events unfold in a film

Rhythm: the pattern of events that creates a sense of continuity and flow in a film

Discuss Different Techniques for Controlling Pace and Rhythm

Use examples from the films provided to illustrate each technique.

Editing: the length of shots and the order in which they're presented

Music and Sound Effects: the tempo, volume, and tone of the soundtrack

Camera Movement: the speed and type of camera movement (e.g., handheld, steady, slow-motion)

Dialogue and Acting: the speed and tone of delivery, the pauses and silences

Analyze Examples from Different Film Genres

Divide the class into groups, each assigned a different genre (e.g., action, romantic, thriller, suspense, horror, sci-fi)

Provide each group with a scene from a film in their genre and ask them to analyze the pace and rhythm of the scene.

Ask each group to present their analysis to the class, discussing how the techniques used in the scene affect the audience's emotions and engagement.

Conclusion:

Review the importance of pace and rhythm in filmmaking and how it affects the audience's emotional response to the film.

Encourage students to think about how they can use these techniques in their own filmmaking projects.

Distribute handouts with the definitions and examples covered in the lesson for students to keep as a reference.

DIRECTING

THE RULE OF THIRDS

As a young filmmaker, it's important to understand the rule of thirds and its true origin and use in filmmaking. The rule of thirds is a compositional technique that involves dividing the frame of a shot into thirds horizontally and vertically, creating a grid of nine equal parts. The rule of thirds suggests placing important visual elements of the shot along these lines or at their intersections, rather than centering them in the frame.

The rule of thirds has its roots in the visual arts, particularly in painting and drawing. Artists have long used the technique to create visually interesting and balanced compositions. In the 18th century, an English painter named John Thomas Smith wrote a book called "Remarks on Rural Scenery" in which he described the rule of thirds as a principle of design in landscape painting.

In filmmaking, the rule of thirds is an important tool for creating visually compelling shots. By placing important elements along the lines and intersections of the grid, filmmakers can create a sense of balance and harmony in the frame. This can help to draw the viewer's eye to important details and create a more dynamic and engaging image.

However, it's important to note that the rule of thirds is not a hard and fast rule. Sometimes, centering an element in the frame can create a powerful and impactful shot. The rule of thirds is simply a guideline that can help filmmakers to create more interesting and balanced compositions.

But what does mathematics have to do with filmmaking and the rule of thirds? Well, filmmaking is a highly technical art form that relies heavily on mathematical concepts such as ratios, angles, and proportions. The rule of thirds is just one example of how mathematical concepts can be used in filmmaking to create more visually interesting shots.

In conclusion, the rule of thirds is a compositional technique that can help young filmmakers to create more visually interesting and balanced shots. While it's important to understand the origins and use of the rule of thirds, it's also important to remember that it's just one tool in a filmmaker's toolbox. By understanding the role that mathematics plays in filmmaking, young filmmakers can develop a more technical and nuanced approach to their craft.

DIRECTING

Blocking and Framing

Title: The Art of Blocking and Movement in Filmmaking

Grade Level: 9-12

Objective: Students will be able to understand the importance of blocking and movement in filmmaking and apply it to create a visually interesting and dynamic scene.

Materials Needed:

Camera

Tripod

Whiteboard

Markers

Script

Lesson Plan:

Introduction (10 mins)

Start the class with a brief discussion about the importance of blocking and movement in filmmaking.

Show a few examples of well-blocked and well-moved scenes from popular movies.

Ask the students if they have any questions or thoughts about the topic.

Instruction (30 mins)

Define blocking and movement and their significance in film.

Explain how blocking and movement can enhance a scene and how it can convey emotion or story elements to the audience.

Discuss different types of camera movement such as pans, tilts, zooms, dolly, and crane shots.

Demonstrate how camera movement can affect the mood, pace, and tension of a scene.

Activity (60 mins)

Divide the class into groups of three or four.

Provide them with a script of a short scene from a popular movie.

Instruct them to read through the script and discuss how they would block and move the actors and the camera to make the scene more visually interesting.

Have each group set up the scene and film it using the camera and tripod.

After each group has finished filming, have them review the footage and analyze what worked and what didn't.

Conclusion (20 mins)

Have each group present their scene to the class.

Ask the students to provide constructive feedback to each other on how they can improve their blocking and movement techniques.

Sum up the lesson by emphasizing the importance of blocking and movement in filmmaking, and how it can elevate a scene and make it more engaging for the audience.

Assessment:

Students will be assessed based on their ability to work collaboratively, apply the concepts of blocking and movement, and create a visually engaging scene

DIRECTING

Blocking and Framing

Blocking and movement are essential techniques in filmmaking that help create a dynamic and engaging scene. Blocking refers to the arrangement and movement of actors within a scene, while movement refers to the camera's movement. Both techniques work together to establish the scene's composition, pace, and emotional tone.

Here are some examples of how blocking and movement are used in filmmaking:

Composition: Blocking and movement can be used to create a visually pleasing and balanced composition. For example, placing actors in specific positions within the frame can create a symmetry that enhances the shot's visual appeal. Movement can also be used to create visual interest, such as tracking the camera's movement as actors move around the frame.

Emotion: The movement of actors can convey specific emotions to the audience. For example, a character walking slowly across the frame can create a sense of sadness or contemplation. Rapid camera movement and quick cuts can create a sense of chaos or urgency.

Pacing: The speed and rhythm of movement can affect the pacing of a scene. For example, slow camera movement and long takes can create a relaxed and reflective mood, while quick camera movement and rapid cuts can create a sense of tension and urgency.

Storytelling: Blocking and movement can also be used to tell a story visually. For example, a close-up shot of a character's hands can suggest their nervousness or anxiety. Movement can also reveal information about the characters or their environment, such as a sudden camera tilt to reveal a threatening character or a pan to show a beautiful landscape.

In summary, the art of blocking and movement in filmmaking is a crucial aspect of creating an engaging and visually appealing scene. The composition, emotion, pacing, and storytelling are all affected by how actors move and how the camera moves within the frame. Understanding and using these techniques can enhance the audience's experience and elevate the film's overall quality.

A SHOT VS SCENE & A SEQUENCE

In filmmaking, a shot refers to a single, continuous take from the camera's perspective. It is the basic building block of a film, and can range in length from just a few seconds to several minutes. Shots are typically framed in a particular way to convey meaning or create a specific visual effect, and can be edited together to create a scene or sequence.

A scene, on the other hand, is a series of shots that are related to each other in terms of time, location, and subject matter. Scenes are typically designed to advance the plot or develop characters, and can range in length from a few seconds to several minutes. They often have a clear beginning, middle, and end, and are usually connected to other scenes to form a larger narrative.

A sequence is a collection of scenes that are related to each other in terms of theme, tone, or narrative structure. Sequences are typically used to create a specific effect or emotion in the audience, and can range in length from a few minutes to several hours. They are often used to transition between different parts of the story, and can be composed of a variety of shots and scenes.

Here's an example to illustrate the difference between a shot, a scene, and a sequence:

Shot: A close-up of a character's face as they react to a surprise revelation.

Scene: A conversation between two characters that takes place in a coffee shop. The scene includes several shots of the characters as they speak, as well as cutaway shots of the environment.

Sequence: A montage of several scenes that show the character processing the new information they learned in the coffee shop. The sequence includes a mix of close-ups, medium shots, and wide shots, as well as a variety of locations and lighting setups.

Quiz:

23. What is a shot in filmmaking? A. A collection of scenes B. A single, continuous take from the camera's perspective C. A series of related shots
24. What is a scene in filmmaking? A. A collection of shots B. A single, continuous take from the camera's perspective C. A series of related shots
25. What is a sequence in filmmaking? A. A single, continuous take from the camera's perspective B. A collection of related shots C. A series of related scenes

Answers:

23. B
24. C
25. B

CINEAMATOGRAPHY

Manual for Camera Operator for Filmmakers

Introduction:

A camera operator is an integral part of the filmmaking process. It is their responsibility to capture the director's vision on film, and it is important that they have a good understanding of how to use the camera to its full potential. This manual will provide some basic tips and techniques for camera operators, as well as some advice on how to work effectively with the rest of the crew.

Cinematography:

Cinematography is the art of capturing visual images on film. It is the job of the cinematographer to work with the director and the rest of the crew to create a visual language that best serves the story. This includes choosing the right camera angles, lighting, and framing techniques to convey emotion, mood, and atmosphere.

Lesson Plan for Shooting a Movie with a Digital Camera vs a Camcorder:

Objective: Students will learn the differences and similarities between shooting with a digital camera and a camcorder, and how to choose the best camera for their project.

Materials:

Digital camera

Camcorder

Tripod

Lighting equipment

Actors (optional)

Procedure:

Introduction to digital cameras and camcorders - Explain the differences between digital cameras and camcorders, including their respective features, strengths, and limitations.

Demonstration of shooting techniques - Demonstrate how to use both a digital camera and a camcorder to shoot a scene, including framing, focusing, and adjusting the lighting.

Camera comparison - Have students shoot the same scene with both a digital camera and a camcorder. Compare the footage and discuss the differences in terms of image quality, color depth, and dynamic range.

Choosing the right camera - Have students work in groups to decide which camera is best for a given project. Have them consider factors such as the intended audience, the tone of the project, and the budget.

Practice - Have students practice shooting scenes with their chosen camera. Encourage them to experiment with different camera angles, lighting setups, and framing techniques.

Critique - Critique the students' footage as a group, and provide feedback on their camera work.

Conclusion:

Shooting a movie requires careful consideration of many factors, including the camera used to capture the footage. By understanding the differences between shooting with a digital camera and a camcorder, and by choosing the right camera for the job, students can produce visually stunning films that effectively convey their stories.

CINEMATOGRAPHY

Camera Features

Digital cameras and camcorders are both devices used for capturing digital video footage, but there are some key differences between the two.

Digital cameras are designed primarily for still photography, but many models also have video recording capabilities. Camcorders, on the other hand, are designed specifically for video recording and often offer more advanced video features.

Features of Digital Cameras:

Aperture: The aperture controls the amount of light that enters the camera lens. A wider aperture (lower f-stop number) allows more light in and can create a shallow depth of field, while a smaller aperture (higher f-stop number) lets in less light and can create a larger depth of field.

Shutter speed: The shutter speed determines how long the camera's sensor is exposed to light. A slower shutter speed allows more light in and can create motion blur, while a faster shutter speed lets in less light and can freeze motion.

ISO: ISO measures the sensitivity of the camera's sensor to light. A higher ISO allows for shooting in low light conditions, but can also introduce digital noise into the image.

Frame rate: Frame rate refers to the number of still images that are captured per second to create a video. Most digital cameras shoot video at 24 or 30 frames per second, although some models can shoot at higher frame rates for slow motion footage.

Features of Camcorders:

Optical zoom: Camcorders typically offer optical zoom lenses, which physically move to zoom in on a subject. This provides higher image quality than digital zoom, which simply crops and enlarges the image.

Continuous autofocus: Camcorders often have more advanced autofocus systems than digital cameras, which can be especially useful for capturing moving subjects.

Audio input: Many camcorders have built-in microphones, as well as input jacks for external microphones. This allows for higher quality audio recording.

Image stabilization: Camcorders often have built-in image stabilization to reduce camera shake and produce smoother footage.

Overall, digital cameras are generally better suited for still photography and casual video recording, while camcorders are designed specifically for video recording and offer more advanced video features. Both types of cameras have their own strengths and limitations, so choosing the right one for a specific project depends on the specific needs and requirements of the project.

CINEMATOGRAPHY

Composing a shot

Composing shots in film refers to the process of framing and positioning the camera and its subjects within the frame. It involves a combination of artistic and technical decisions, including choosing the camera angle, the distance of the camera from the subject, and the placement of the subject within the frame.

Spatial connections in cinematography refer to the way that the camera and its subjects are positioned within the frame in relation to one another. This can include the use of foreground, middle ground, and background elements to create depth and perspective, as well as the positioning of the camera and the subject to create a sense of balance and symmetry.

Here are some examples of how spatial connections can be used in cinematography to create compelling shots:

26. Rule of Thirds: This technique involves dividing the frame into thirds both horizontally and vertically, and positioning the subject along one of these lines or at their intersection. This creates a sense of balance and can make the shot more visually appealing.
27. Foreground Elements: By placing objects or people in the foreground of the shot, filmmakers can create a sense of depth and perspective. This can also help to draw the viewer's eye to the subject.
28. High Angle Shots: This involves positioning the camera above the subject, looking down on them. This can create a sense of vulnerability or weakness, as well as making the subject appear smaller and less important.
29. Low Angle Shots: This involves positioning the camera below the subject, looking up at them. This can create a sense of power or dominance, as well as making the subject appear larger and more important.
30. Dutch Angle: This involves tilting the camera to one side, creating a sense of unease or disorientation. This can be used to create a sense of tension or chaos in a scene.

Overall, composing shots and using spatial connections in cinematography is an essential part of filmmaking. It allows filmmakers to create a sense of mood, perspective, and emotion, and can help to draw the viewer deeper into the story.

WHAT IS CINEMATOGPAAHY

Cinematography refers to the art and technique of capturing moving images on film or digitally. It involves a range of technical and creative decisions, including camera placement, framing, lighting, and color grading, all with the goal of creating a visually compelling and emotionally engaging image.

The history of cinematography dates back to the late 19th century, when pioneers such as Eadweard Muybridge and Thomas Edison began experimenting with motion picture cameras. In the early 20th century, filmmakers such as D.W. Griffith and Sergei Eisenstein began using cinematography to tell stories in new and innovative ways, using techniques such as cross-cutting and montage to create a sense of tension and drama.

Throughout the 20th century, cinematography continued to evolve and innovate, with new technologies such as sound recording, color film, and digital cameras allowing filmmakers to create increasingly complex and immersive visual experiences.

Some of the most notable cinematographers in the history of filmmaking include:

31. Gregg Toland: Known for his work on films such as Citizen Kane and The Grapes of Wrath, Toland was a pioneer in the use of deep focus and wide-angle lenses.
32. Vittorio Storaro: With a career spanning over five decades, Storaro is known for his work on films such as Apocalypse Now, The Last Emperor, and Reds. He is known for his use of color and light to create bold and vibrant images.
33. Gordon Willis: Often referred to as the "Prince of Darkness," Willis was known for his work on films such as The Godfather and Annie Hall, and for his use of shadows and low lighting to create a sense of atmosphere and mood.
34. Roger Deakins: With 15 Oscar nominations and three wins to his name, Deakins is one of the most highly

regarded cinematographers working today. He is known for his work on films such as Blade Runner 2049, Skyfall, and No Country for Old Men.

To improve your own skills as a cinematographer, it's important to study the work of other filmmakers and cinematographers, experiment with different camera techniques and lighting setups, and continue to refine your craft through practice and experimentation. It can also be helpful to seek out feedback from other filmmakers and professionals in the industry, and to stay up-to-date with the latest trends and technologies in the field.

CINEMATOGRAPHY

Staging and shooting dialogue

Staging dialogue for the camera in filmmaking is a crucial aspect of creating a visually compelling and emotionally engaging movie. There are several techniques and approaches that filmmakers can use to effectively stage dialogue and capture the best possible performance from their actors. Here are some tips and techniques for staging dialogue for the camera:

35. Blocking: Blocking refers to the movement and positioning of actors within a scene. By carefully choreographing the movements of actors, filmmakers can create a sense of visual interest and depth within a scene, as well as draw attention to key moments of dialogue or action. It's important to consider factors such as eyelines, proximity, and screen direction when blocking a scene.
36. Camera placement: The placement of the camera is another crucial factor in staging dialogue. Depending on the desired effect, filmmakers may choose to use a wide shot to establish the scene and the characters within it, or a close-up to focus on the facial expressions and emotions of the actors. By experimenting with different camera

angles and placements, filmmakers can create a sense of visual variety and interest within a scene.
37. Shot/reverse shot: Shot/reverse shot is a classic technique used in filming dialogue scenes. It involves alternating shots between two characters, with each shot focusing on the character who is speaking. This technique creates a sense of visual continuity and allows the audience to follow the flow of the conversation.
38. Sequences and patterns: Sequences and patterns are another important aspect of staging dialogue for the camera. By carefully planning the sequence of shots within a scene, filmmakers can create a sense of rhythm and momentum that enhances the emotional impact of the dialogue. Patterns such as shot/reverse shot or over-the-shoulder shots can also help create a sense of visual continuity and coherence within a scene.

When it comes to shooting dialogue for a movie using a cell phone, digital camera, or camcorder, many of the same principles of staging and camera placement still apply. However, there are a few additional considerations to keep in mind. For example:

39. Lighting: When shooting with a cell phone or digital camera, lighting is especially important. Make sure to position the actors in a well-lit area, and consider using artificial lighting if necessary to create the desired effect.
40. Audio: Audio quality is another key consideration when shooting dialogue with a cell phone or digital camera. Consider using an external microphone to capture clearer, more nuanced sound, and be mindful of any background noise that could interfere with the dialogue.
41. Stability: With a cell phone or digital camera, it's important to ensure that the camera is stable and steady throughout the scene. Consider using a tripod or stabilizer to minimize shaky or unsteady footage.

Overall, staging dialogue for the camera in filmmaking requires careful attention to detail and a keen eye for visual storytelling. By experimenting with different techniques and approaches, filmmakers can create scenes that are both visually compelling and emotionally engaging for audiences.

CINEMATOGRAPHY

Techniques for shooting a movie with tracking shots and dolly shots using an iPhone or late model android to get clear and smooth footage:

42. Use a stabilizing rig: Stabilizing rigs such as gimbals can help eliminate camera shake, resulting in smoother footage.
43. Plan out the shot: Determine the path the camera will take and make sure the actors are aware of it. This will ensure that the shot is executed smoothly.
44. Use a tripod or monopod: A tripod or monopod can provide stability for your shot, making it easier to get a smooth shot.
45. Use a slider: A slider allows you to create smooth tracking shots.
46. Use slow movement: Moving the camera too quickly can result in shaky footage. Slow and steady movements can help achieve a smoother shot.
47. Shoot in 4k: Shooting in 4k will give you more resolution to work with, allowing you to stabilize the footage in post-production.

How to avoid shaking footage:

48. Use a stabilizing rig: A stabilizing rig such as a gimbal can help eliminate camera shake.
49. Use a tripod or monopod: Using a tripod or monopod can provide stability for your shot, reducing camera shake.

50. Hold the camera with two hands: Holding the camera with two hands can help stabilize the shot.
51. Use slow movements: Moving the camera too quickly can result in shaky footage. Slow and steady movements can help achieve a smoother shot.
52. Use image stabilization: Some cameras have built-in image stabilization, which can help reduce camera shake.

Difference between a tripod, monopod, gimbal, and steady cam:

53. Tripod: A tripod is a three-legged stand used to support a camera. It provides stability and allows for still shots.
54. Monopod: A monopod is a one-legged stand used to support a camera. It provides some stability, but not as much as a tripod.
55. Gimbal: A gimbal is a device that allows the camera to rotate on multiple axes while keeping it level. It provides stability and allows for smooth movements.
56. Steadicam: A Steadicam is a camera stabilization system that uses a vest and arm to support the camera. It allows for smooth movements and can be used for longer shots.

CINEMATOGRAPHY

Shooting a film with a mobile phone only

Lesson Plan: Shooting a Script for a Movie with Fast-Paced Action Using a Cell Phone and Shotgun Microphone

Objective: Students will learn how to shoot a fast-paced action scene using a cell phone and shotgun microphone.

Materials:

- Cell phone with video recording capabilities
- Shotgun microphone
- Tripod or stabilizing rig

- Script with a fast-paced action scene

Procedure:

Introduction (15 minutes):

57. Discuss the importance of shooting fast-paced action scenes in movies and how it can add to the excitement and tension of a scene.
58. Introduce the equipment that will be used in the lesson, including the cell phone, shotgun microphone, and stabilizing rig.
59. Go over the script with the class and discuss the important elements of the action scene that they will be shooting.

Demonstration (30 minutes):

60. Demonstrate how to set up the equipment, including attaching the shotgun microphone to the cell phone and mounting it on the tripod or stabilizing rig.
61. Show how to frame the shots and position the camera for the best angles and perspectives.
62. Demonstrate how to adjust the settings on the cell phone camera, including the exposure and focus, to get the best results.

Practice (60 minutes):

63. Divide the class into small groups and assign them a scene to shoot from the script.
64. Have students work together to set up the equipment and plan out the shots for their scene.
65. Students will then shoot their scene, paying close attention to framing, camera movement, and sound quality.
66. After each group has shot their scene, they will review the footage and provide feedback to each other.

Conclusion (15 minutes):

67. Review the footage with the class and discuss the strengths and weaknesses of each scene.
68. Discuss how the use of a shotgun microphone can improve the sound quality of the footage, especially in a fast-paced action scene.
69. Encourage students to continue practicing their skills and experimenting with different camera techniques and equipment to improve their filmmaking abilities.

DIRECTING

What Film Editing a Film

Editing is the process of selecting and combining raw footage to create a finished film. It involves many techniques and styles that have evolved over the years, each with its own unique impact on the final product.

One of the earliest and most influential editing techniques is the montage, which involves the rapid intercutting of images to convey a specific idea or emotion. This technique was popularized by Russian filmmaker Sergei Eisenstein and has been used in countless films since.

Another common editing technique is B-roll, which involves the use of supplementary footage to provide context or visual interest during transitions or to cover cuts in dialogue. This can include shots of the environment, people, or objects related to the subject matter.

Cutting on action is a technique that involves cutting from one shot to another during an action or movement, creating a sense of continuity and fluidity. Juxtaposition is a technique that involves placing contrasting or complementary shots side by side to create a specific effect, such as highlighting a character's emotions or creating tension.

Point of view editing involves cutting between shots that show what a character is seeing or experiencing to put the viewer in their shoes. Tonal montage is a technique that involves creating a specific emotional or tonal effect through the use of carefully selected shots and edits.

Eye trace is a technique that involves ensuring that the viewer's attention follows the intended path of the action or story, by controlling the direction of characters' movements and the placement of objects within the frame.

One of the most important factors in editing is the duration of a shot. Research by film editor Walter Murch suggests that the optimal duration of a shot is around 2-3 seconds, as this is the average length of a person's blink. This can vary depending on the desired effect, but it's important to keep the viewer engaged and avoid any sense of boredom or fatigue.

To edit a film, you will need a video editing software such as Adobe Premiere, Final Cut Pro or DaVinci Resolve. Start by importing all of your footage into the software and organizing it into bins or folders. Then, create a rough cut by selecting the best shots and arranging them in a logical order.

Once you have a rough cut, you can refine it by adding transitions, effects, and sound. You can also adjust the timing of individual shots to create the desired pacing and rhythm. Continuously review your work and make adjustments until you are satisfied with the final product.

Quiz:

70. What is the purpose of a montage in film editing?

a) To show supplementary footage

b) To create a specific emotional or tonal effect

c) To rapidly intercut images to convey a specific idea or emotion

d) To ensure that the viewer's attention follows the intended path of the action or story

Answer: c) To rapidly intercut images to convey a specific idea or emotion

71. What is the optimal duration of a shot according to Walter Murch's research?

a) 5-6 seconds

b) 2-3 seconds

c) 1-2 seconds

d) 10-12 seconds

Answer: b) 2-3 seconds

72. What is the purpose of cutting on action in film editing?

a) To create a specific emotional or tonal effect

b) To rapidly intercut images to convey a specific idea or emotion

c) To place contrasting or complementary shots side by side to create a specific effect

d) To create a sense of continuity and fluidity

Answer: d) To create a sense of continuity and fluidity

FILM EDITING

Sergei Eisenstein's theory of montage is a film editing technique that involves the juxtaposition of different shots to create a new meaning or idea. Montage is the process of assembling different shots or scenes in a way that conveys a particular message or emotion.

Instructions for Editing a Film using Eisenstein's Theory of Montage:

- Analyze the script and identify the key themes and ideas that need to be conveyed through the film.
- Choose the appropriate shots or scenes that will help convey the message or emotion.
- Decide on the type of montage that will be used to convey the message effectively.
- Juxtapose the shots or scenes in a specific order to create the desired effect.
- Use sound, music, and other effects to enhance the impact of the montage.
- Types of Montage:

Metric Montage: This type of montage uses the length of the shots to create a sense of rhythm and pattern. It is based on the length of the shots and their duration. For example, a series of quick shots can be used to convey a sense of urgency or tension.

Rhythmic Montage: This type of montage uses the movement and pace of the shots to create a sense of rhythm and pattern. It is based on the movement of the characters or objects within the shots. For example, a series of shots that show the characters walking in unison can be used to create a sense of unity or teamwork.

Tonal Montage: This type of montage uses the emotional content of the shots to create a specific tone or mood. It is based on the emotional content of the shots and their impact on the viewer. For example, a series of sad and melancholic shots can be used to create a somber mood.

Over tonal montage: This type of montage is similar to tonal montage but uses contrasting images to create a new meaning or emotion. It is based on the juxtaposition of different emotions to create a new emotional experience. For example, a sad shot can be juxtaposed with a happy shot to create a sense of irony or contrast.

Intellectual Montage: This type of montage uses the shots to convey a specific message or idea. It is based on the ideas or concepts that are presented in the shots. For example, a series of shots that show poverty, hunger, and homelessness can be used to convey a message about social inequality.

Visual Discontinuity: This type of montage uses the sudden and abrupt changes in the shots to create a sense of surprise or shock. It is based on the sudden shift in the visual elements of the shots. For example, a series of shots that show a peaceful countryside scene can be suddenly interrupted by a shot of a violent storm to create a sense of surprise or shock.

Overall, the key to using Eisenstein's theory of montage is to understand the desired message or emotion and choose the appropriate type of montage to convey it effectively. The editing process should be carefully planned and executed to create a cohesive and impactful film.

FILM EDITING ACTIVITY

Title: Film Editing Workshop: Exploring Eisenstein's Theory of Montage

Objectives:

To understand the basic principles of film editing using Eisenstein's theory of montage

To explore the different types of montage: Metric, Rhythmic, Tonal, Over Tonal, Intellectual, and Visual Discontinuity

To practice and apply the different types of montage to edit a short film

Materials:

Laptops with video editing software (e.g. iMovie, Adobe Premiere)

Short film footage (can be downloaded from online sources)

Projector and screen

Handouts on Eisenstein's theory of montage

Duration: 3 hours

Activity 1: Introduction (15 minutes)

Welcome the participants and give a brief introduction to Eisenstein's theory of montage

Distribute handouts and explain the different types of montage

Show examples of each type of montage in films

Activity 2: Film Editing Exercise (60 minutes)

Divide the participants into small groups and assign them a specific type of montage (Metric, Rhythmic, Tonal, Over Tonal, Intellectual, or Visual Discontinuity)

Provide the groups with short film footage and laptops with video editing software

Instruct the groups to edit the footage using their assigned type of montage

Encourage the groups to experiment with different shots and sounds to create a cohesive and impactful montage

Activity 3: Group Presentation (45 minutes)

After the editing exercise, ask each group to present their edited film to the rest of the participants

Allow time for feedback and discussion on the effectiveness of each type of montage

Activity 4: Reflection and Wrap-Up (30 minutes)

Ask the participants to reflect on their experience and share their thoughts on the different types of montage

Summarize the key points discussed in the workshop and highlight the importance of planning and execution in film editing

Provide resources for further learning on Eisenstein's theory of montage and film editing

Assessment:

The participants' edited films will be assessed based on their use and effectiveness of the assigned type of montage.

Feedback and discussion during the presentation will also be considered in the assessment.

Overall, this workshop aims to introduce young adults to the principles of film editing using Eisenstein's theory of montage. By practicing and applying the different types of montage, the participants will gain a better understanding of the impact of editing on the storytelling process in film.

FILM EDITING TECHNIQUES

Film editing techniques are the methods and approaches used by filmmakers to manipulate the visual and audio elements of a film in order to tell a story, create emotions, and engage the audience. Here are some examples of film editing techniques using scenarios from Alfred Hitchcock's films:

Parallel Action - This technique involves cutting between two or more different scenes happening simultaneously. For example, in Alfred Hitchcock's film "North by Northwest," the scene where the protagonist is chased by a crop duster while a bus is approaching from the other direction is a classic example of parallel action.

The Sound Cut - This technique involves the sudden shift or interruption of audio within a scene. In Hitchcock's "Psycho," the sound of the shower curtain being ripped open is abruptly interrupted by the sound of the stabbing knife, creating a shocking and memorable effect.

Cutting on Motion - This technique involves cutting to a new shot while there is still motion in the previous shot. For example, in Hitchcock's "Vertigo," the camera tracks in towards the protagonist's face while cutting to a close-up shot of his eye, creating a sense of tension and unease.

Suspense: The Extreme Long Shot - This technique involves showing a distant, wide shot of a scene to create suspense and anticipation. In Hitchcock's "The Birds," the extreme long shot of the birds gathering outside the protagonist's house creates a sense of impending danger.

The Meaning of Cutaway - This technique involves cutting away from the main action to show a detail or reaction shot that adds meaning or context to the scene. For example, in Hitchcock's "Psycho," the cutaway to the showerhead immediately after the murder adds a layer of symbolism and meaning to the scene.

Intensity: Close-Up - This technique involves showing a close-up shot of a character or object to create intensity and focus. In Hitchcock's "Vertigo," the close-up shots of the protagonist's face and eyes help to convey his inner turmoil and psychological state.

Unity of Sound - This technique involves using sound to create a cohesive and unified atmosphere throughout a film. In

Hitchcock's "Rear Window," the sound of the city and the various neighbors' activities help to create a sense of unity and interconnectedness within the film's setting.

Dream States and Subjectivity - This technique involves using visual and audio cues to convey a character's dreams or subjective experiences. In Hitchcock's "Spellbound," the use of surreal imagery and subjective camera angles helps to convey the protagonist's dreamlike state of mind.

Motion - This technique involves using camera movement to create a sense of motion and dynamic energy within a scene. In Hitchcock's "Psycho," the camera movement during the shower scene adds to the chaotic and violent nature of the scene.

By understanding and utilizing these different film editing techniques, young adults can create more engaging and impactful films that capture the attention and emotions of their audiences.

VARIOUS FORMS OF FILMMAKING

Discussion: Making Films with Artificial Reality, Video over Film, Spectacle, Special Effects, and Virtual Film Production

Today we are going to discuss the various techniques and technologies that filmmakers use to create their movies, including artificial reality, video over film, spectacle, special effects, and virtual film production. Let's start by defining each of these terms.

Artificial reality refers to the use of computer-generated images and animations to create a world that appears real but is entirely digital. This technique has been used in films like "Avatar" (2009) and "Ready Player One" (2018) to create immersive and fantastical worlds that would be impossible to film in reality.

Video over film is a technique where filmmakers shoot their movie using digital cameras instead of traditional film cameras. This method has become increasingly popular in recent years due to the ease and cost-effectiveness of digital filming, as well as the ability to edit and manipulate footage more easily in post-production.

Spectacle refers to the use of grand and impressive visuals and effects to create a sense of awe and wonder in the audience. This technique has been used in films like "Interstellar" (2014) and "Inception" (2010) to create visually stunning and mind-bending sequences.

Special effects refer to the use of practical or digital techniques to create visual illusions or enhance a scene. Examples of practical effects include makeup, prosthetics, and animatronics, while digital effects include computer-generated imagery (CGI) and motion graphics. These techniques have been used in countless films, from the practical effects of "Jurassic Park" (1993) to the digital effects of "The Avengers" (2012).

Virtual film production involves the use of digital environments and techniques to shoot and create a film entirely in a computer-generated world. This technique has become increasingly popular in recent years, with films like "The Lion King" (2019) and "The Mandalorian" (2019) using virtual production to create their stunning and immersive worlds.

Now that we have defined these techniques, let's discuss how they can be used effectively in storytelling.

Artificial reality can be used to create fantastical worlds and creatures that would be impossible to film in reality, allowing filmmakers to explore new and exciting ideas and themes. For example, in "Avatar," director James Cameron created an entire world with its own culture, language, and creatures, allowing the audience to fully immerse themselves in this new and unique universe.

Video over film can be used to create a more naturalistic and authentic feel to a film, allowing the audience to feel more connected to the characters and story. This technique was used in "Manchester by the Sea" (2016), which was shot entirely on digital cameras to create a raw and emotional atmosphere.

Spectacle can be used to create a sense of awe and wonder in the audience, adding to the emotional impact of a scene. For example, in "Interstellar," director Christopher Nolan used stunning visual effects to depict the wonders of space and the awe-inspiring nature of the universe.

Special effects can be used to enhance a scene or create an illusion that would be impossible to achieve otherwise. In "Jurassic Park," director Steven Spielberg used groundbreaking practical effects to bring the dinosaurs to life, creating a sense of realism and wonder in the audience.

Virtual film production can be used to create entire worlds and environments, allowing filmmakers to explore new ideas and create entirely unique visual experiences. In "The Mandalorian," virtual production was used to create the stunning and immersive world of the Star Wars universe, allowing the audience to fully immerse themselves in this beloved universe.

In conclusion, the techniques and technologies used to create films are constantly evolving and changing, allowing filmmakers to push the boundaries of what is possible in storytelling. By understanding

SOUND

When it comes to recording sound for a movie, there are several types of microphones that can be used. The two most common types are shotgun microphones and wireless microphones.

Shotgun microphones are directional microphones that are designed to capture sound from a specific direction while rejecting sound from other directions. They are often used on movie sets to capture dialogue and other important sounds. To use a shotgun microphone effectively, it should be positioned as close to the sound source as possible without appearing in the shot. It should also be aimed directly at the sound source to ensure the best possible sound quality.

Wireless microphones are another popular option for recording sound on a movie set. They are typically worn by actors and can be concealed in their clothing or hair to provide a more natural sound. However, they can be prone to interference from other devices, so it's important to choose a high-quality wireless microphone and test it thoroughly before shooting.

When recording sound for a movie, it's important to avoid background noise as much as possible. This can be accomplished by choosing a quiet location to shoot, using sound-absorbing materials like blankets or acoustic foam, and minimizing movement during recording. It's also important to use headphones to monitor the sound while recording to ensure that unwanted noise is not being picked up by the microphone.

In terms of where to place and hide microphones on a movie set, it's important to think creatively and strategically. For example, a microphone can be hidden in a plant or behind a piece of furniture to capture sound without being seen. It's also important to test different positions and angles to find the best placement for each microphone.

Overall, capturing high-quality sound for a movie requires careful planning, attention to detail, and the right equipment.

With the right microphone and placement, it's possible to achieve excellent sound quality and create a more immersive and engaging movie experience for viewers.

2D Cartooning 12 Principles of Animation

The 12 principles of animation were first introduced by Disney animators Ollie Johnston and Frank Thomas in their book "The Illusion of Life." These principles provide a set of guidelines for animators to create believable and appealing animations. Here are the 12 principles of animation and a brief description of each:

1. Squash and Stretch: This principle involves deforming an object to show its weight and movement. For example, a bouncing ball will stretch when it hits the ground and squash when it bounces back up.
2. Anticipation: Anticipation is used to prepare the viewer for an action. For example, a character may look back before running away from danger.
3. Staging: This principle is about presenting the action in a clear and understandable way. It involves framing the shot, placing the camera, and arranging the characters in the scene.
4. Straight Ahead Action and Pose to Pose: These are two different approaches to animating. Straight Ahead Action involves drawing each frame in sequence, while Pose to Pose involves creating key poses and then filling in the in-between frames.
5. Follow Through and Overlapping Action: These principles involve adding secondary motion to an action. For example, the hair of a running character will continue to move after the character has stopped.
6. Slow In and Slow Out: This principle involves starting and stopping an action gradually to make it appear more natural.
7. Arcs: Most movements follow an arc, such as a swinging pendulum or a ball thrown in the air. Animators use arcs to make movements appear more natural.

8. Secondary Action: This principle involves adding a secondary action to the main action. For example, a character may scratch their head while thinking.
9. Timing: Timing is about determining the speed and timing of actions to create a sense of realism and weight.
10. Exaggeration: This principle involves exaggerating certain movements to make them more appealing and entertaining.
11. Solid Drawing: This principle involves creating drawings that have a sense of weight and volume, and appear three-dimensional.
12. Appeal: Appeal is about creating characters and designs that are appealing and attractive to the audience.

To apply these principles in 2D animation, animators must first plan out the animation by creating a storyboard and animatic. Then, they can begin animating using traditional techniques such as hand-drawn animation, or digital techniques using software such as Adobe Animate or Toon Boom Harmony.

Here are 12 examples of how the 12 principles of animation can be applied in 2D animation:

1. Squash and Stretch: A bouncing ball or a character jumping.
2. Anticipation: A character winding up before throwing a punch.
3. Staging: Placing a character in the foreground to draw attention to them.
4. Straight Ahead Action and Pose to Pose: Straight Ahead Action for a fast action scene and Pose to Pose for a more deliberate scene.
5. Follow Through and Overlapping Action: The hair of a character flows after they turn their head.
6. Slow In and Slow Out: A character gradually standing up from a chair.
7. Arcs: A character swinging a baseball bat.
8. Secondary Action: A character blinking while talking.

9. Timing: A character runs slowly when they're tired, and runs quickly when they're scared.
10. Exaggeration: A character's facial expression when they're surprised.
11. Solid Drawing: A character's body twisting and bending as they walk.
12. Appeal: Creating a character with unique features that are visually interesting.

Here's a lesson plan for teaching teens and young adults the 12 principles of animation:

Lesson Title: The 12 Principles of Animation

Objective: Students will learn the 12 principles of animation and apply them in a short 2

CHARACTER DEVELOPMENT

Character development is a crucial aspect of creating compelling and memorable characters for TV or film. In this guide, we will explore the key elements of character development, including character arc, character style, character types, and provide examples for both 2D and 3D films.

Character Arc: A character arc refers to the transformation of a character throughout the story. This transformation can be positive or negative, and it is an essential component of character development. A character arc typically includes three stages: the beginning, middle, and end.

Beginning: The beginning of a character arc establishes the character's personality, desires, and motivations. This stage sets up the character's journey and the conflicts they will face.

Middle: The middle of a character arc is where the character faces challenges and undergoes transformation. This stage is where the character begins to change and grow as a result of their experiences.

End: The end of a character arc is where the character has completed their transformation. This stage should show how the character has changed and how they have grown as a result of their journey.

Character Style: Character style refers to the visual appearance of a character, including their clothing, hair, and makeup. Character style can be used to communicate a character's personality and traits. There are several pros and cons to consider when developing a character style.

Pros:

Character style can help differentiate characters and make them memorable.

Character style can help communicate a character's personality and traits to the audience.

Cons:

Character style can be difficult and time-consuming to develop.

If the character style is not well-executed, it can be distracting and take away from the story.

Character Types: There are several types of characters that can be used in TV or film, each with their own strengths and weaknesses. Here are some examples of character types:

Protagonist: The protagonist is the main character in the story. They are typically the hero or heroine and are the character that the audience is meant to root for.

Antagonist: The antagonist is the character who opposes the protagonist. They are typically the villain and provide obstacles for the protagonist to overcome.

Supporting Characters: Supporting characters are characters who help or hinder the protagonist. They can be friends, family members, or other characters who are instrumental in the protagonist's journey.

Foil Characters: Foil characters are characters who are the opposite of the protagonist. They are often used to highlight the protagonist's strengths and weaknesses.

2D Film Example: In the classic Disney film, The Lion King, the protagonist, Simba, undergoes a character arc from an immature and carefree cub to a responsible and courageous leader. His character style evolves from a playful and innocent cub to a majestic and powerful lion. The supporting characters, such as Nala and Timon and Pumbaa, provide comic relief and emotional support for Simba.

3D Film Example: In the Pixar film, Toy Story, the protagonist, Woody, undergoes a character arc from a jealous and possessive toy to a selfless and loyal friend. His character style is that of a classic cowboy, complete with a hat, boots, and a sheriff badge. The antagonist, Buzz Lightyear, provides the obstacle for Woody to overcome, and the supporting characters, such as Mr. Potato Head and Rex, provide comic relief and emotional support.

In conclusion, character development is an essential component of creating memorable and compelling characters for TV or film. A well-executed character arc, character style, and character types can help communicate a character's personality, desires, and motivations to the audience. By understanding the key elements of character development and using examples from 2D and 3D films, writers and filmmakers can create characters that resonate with audiences and leave a lasting impression.

write a class lesson on character development for 2d and 3d animation discuss character arc with examples of life to death, rich to poor, cowardly hearted to courageous, drunk to sober, make to female, and explain character styles like realistic, stylized, idealized, exaggerated, abstract, symbolic, cartoony and discuss the pros and cons and the internal character attributes like fearful, addiction, age and gender or animal or a fruit or vegetable and the way they speak.

Class Lesson: Character Development for 2D and 3D Animation

Introduction: Character development is an essential part of creating compelling and memorable characters in animation. In this lesson, we will explore the key elements of character development in 2D and 3D animation, including character arc, character styles, and internal character attributes.

Character Arc: A character arc is the transformation of a character throughout the story. It is a critical element of character development that can make the character more relatable and interesting to the audience. There are several types of character arcs, including life to death, rich to poor, cowardly to courageous, drunk to sober, and male to female.

Examples of Character Arcs:

Life to Death: In the movie Coco, the protagonist, Miguel, starts as a young boy who loves music but is forbidden by his family to pursue it. Through his journey to the Land of the Dead, he learns about his family's history and the importance of family. In the end, he returns to the Land of the Living as a young man who has found his passion for music and reconciled with his family.

Rich to Poor: In the classic Disney movie Aladdin, the titular character starts as a street urchin who dreams of a better life. Through his adventures with Princess Jasmine and Genie, he learns that true happiness comes from love and friendship, not material wealth.

Cowardly to Courageous: In the movie How to Train Your Dragon, the protagonist, Hiccup, starts as a weak and fearful Viking who wants to prove himself to his father. Through his friendship with Toothless, a dragon, he learns about compassion and bravery, becoming a courageous leader who saves his village from a dragon attack.

Character Styles: Character styles refer to the visual appearance of a character, including their clothing, hair, and makeup. There are several types of character styles, including realistic, stylized, idealized, exaggerated, abstract, symbolic, and cartoony.

Pros and Cons of Character Styles:

Realistic: Pros: Characters can be very relatable and realistic. Cons: Realistic characters can be time-consuming and expensive to create.

Stylized: Pros: Characters can be unique and interesting. Cons: Stylized characters may not be relatable to the audience.

Idealized: Pros: Characters can be aspirational and desirable. Cons: Idealized characters may be unrealistic and unattainable.

Exaggerated: Pros: Characters can be expressive and humorous. Cons: Exaggerated characters may not be realistic or relatable.

Abstract: Pros: Characters can be creative and unique. Cons: Abstract characters may not be recognizable or relatable to the audience.

Symbolic: Pros: Characters can represent abstract ideas or concepts. Cons: Symbolic characters may not be relatable to the audience.

Cartoony: Pros: Characters can be humorous and playful. Cons: Cartoony characters may not be realistic or relatable.

Internal Character Attributes: Internal character attributes refer to a character's personality, fears, strengths, weaknesses, and other internal traits. These attributes can make the character more relatable and interesting to the audience. Some internal character attributes include fearfulness, addiction

CHARACTER DEVELOPMENT

Introduction:

Character development is an essential aspect of creating memorable and relatable characters in TV and film. In this lesson, we will explore the different elements of character development, including place of origin, behavior, speech, style, human or animal, age, and gender. We will also engage in several activities to help you develop your own characters.

Activity 1: Place of Origin

Ask the students to choose a place of origin for their character, whether it's a country, state, city, or neighborhood. Have them research the culture, customs, and traditions of the place they chose and encourage them to incorporate those elements into their character's background and personality.

Activity 2: Behavior

Ask the students to choose a behavior or mannerism for their character, such as a nervous tick, a habit of biting their nails, or a tendency to talk too much. Have them think about how this behavior can reveal something about the character's personality or backstory.

Activity 3: Speech

Ask the students to choose a speech pattern for their character, such as an accent or a way of speaking that's unique to their character. Have them think about how this speech pattern can reveal something about the character's place of origin or personality.

Activity 4: Style

Ask the students to choose a style for their character, whether it's a fashion style or a design style. Have them think about how this style can reflect something about the character's personality or backstory.

Activity 5: Human or Animal

Ask the students to choose whether their character is a human or an animal. If they choose an animal, have them think about how the animal's characteristics can reflect something about the character's personality or backstory.

Activity 6: Age and Gender

Ask the students to choose an age and gender for their character. Have them think about how these factors can shape the character's personality, backstory, and relationships with other characters.

Conclusion:

Character development is a complex process that involves many different elements, from a place of origin to behavior to age and gender. By engaging in these activities, students can develop well-rounded and memorable characters that will engage and resonate with audiences. Encourage them to think creatively and outside the box, and remind them that the best characters are often the ones that are the most unique and unexpected.

ART DIRECTION

Art Direction for 2D and 3D Films and Live Action Movies

Art direction is a crucial aspect of creating visually stunning films. It involves determining the style, design, and mood of a film and bringing it to life through various elements like matte paintings, weather, background, lighting, texture, and environment. In this lesson, we will discuss how to come up with an art direction style and mood for 2D and 3D films as well as live-action movies.

Step 1: Determine the Style

The first step in coming up with an art direction style is to determine the overall look and feel of the film. You can choose from a range of styles like realism, highly realistic, semi-realistic, cartoony, abstract, and symbolic. Consider the genre and tone of the film and choose a style that complements it. For example, a fantasy film might benefit from a highly realistic style, while a comedy might benefit from a cartoony style.

Step 2: Design Elements

Next, you'll need to consider the design elements of the film, including character design, set design, and prop design. Think about how these elements can contribute to the overall style and mood of the film. For example, a character's costume design can help communicate their personality or status in society.

Step 3: Matte Paintings

Matte paintings are static, painted backdrops that can be used to create expansive and detailed environments that would be impractical to build or film. Consider using matte paintings to help establish the setting and mood of your film.

Step 4: Weather and Background

Weather and background can be used to further establish the mood of a film. Think about how different weather conditions can affect the look and feel of a scene. For example, a dark and stormy night might be used to create a sense of foreboding.

Step 5: Lighting and Texture

Lighting and texture can be used to create a sense of depth and realism in a film. Consider how different lighting and texture techniques can help establish the mood and tone of a scene. For example, harsh lighting can be used to create tension or suspense, while soft lighting can be used to create a sense of romance or nostalgia.

Step 6: Color Palette

Finally, you'll need to consider the color palette of the film. Choose colors that complement the overall style and mood of the film. For example, warm colors like red, orange, and yellow might be used to create a sense of energy and excitement, while cool colors like blue and green might be used to create a sense of calm or melancholy.

Examples of Art Direction and Style:

Realism: The film "The Revenant" uses a highly realistic style to create a gritty and immersive experience.

Highly Realistic: The film "Avatar" uses cutting-edge technology to create a stunningly realistic and immersive world.

Semi-Realistic: The Pixar film "Up" uses a semi-realistic style to create a colorful and whimsical world.

Cartoony: The Disney film "Moana" uses a cartoony style to create a vibrant and energetic world.

Abstract and Symbolic: The film "Eternal Sunshine of the Spotless Mind" uses an abstract and symbolic style to create a dreamlike and surreal experience.

Finding and Developing Color Palettes:

When developing a color palette, consider using online tools like Adobe Color to help you experiment with different color combinations. Think about how color can be used to communicate emotion and tone and choose colors that complement the overall style and mood of the film. For example, warm colors like red and orange might be used to create a sense of energy and excitement, while cool colors like blue and green might be used to create a sense of calm.

PRODUCTION PLANNING

Production planning is an essential part of creating a 2D or 3D film. To ensure the smooth execution of the film project, various charts and elements are used in the production planning process. Here are some examples:

Storyboards: Storyboards are visual representations of the script or screenplay, where the scenes are illustrated through rough sketches. Storyboards help in organizing the visual flow of the film and can be used to convey ideas to the production team.

Animatics: Animatics are rough animated versions of the storyboard, which show the movement and timing of the characters and objects in a scene. Animatics can help the director and production team to see how the story will unfold in real-time.

Layouts: Layouts are the detailed drawings of the scenes, including camera angles, lighting, and backgrounds. They provide a blueprint for the final scenes and help in planning the animation and camera movements.

Shot Progress Chart: A Shot Progress Chart is a visual representation of the progress of each shot in the film. It shows the status of each shot, including whether it's in the storyboard stage, layout stage, animation stage, or final rendering stage.

Global Shot Schedule: A Global Shot Schedule is an overview of the entire film production, showing the order in which shots will be created, their status, and deadlines for completion.

Props: Props are objects that the characters interact with in a scene. A list of props is created in the pre-production stage, and they are created during the production stage.

Music: Music is an integral part of a film, and a music cue sheet is created to indicate the timing and placement of music in each scene.

Budget: A budget chart is used to keep track of the budget for the film, including expenses such as equipment, location rentals, and salaries.

Release Forms: Release Forms are signed by talent and locations, granting permission to use their likeness or property in the film.

Example: Let's say we are creating a 3D animated film. In the pre-production stage, we would create a storyboard, animatic, and layout for each scene. We would also create a shot progress chart to track the progress of each shot and a global shot schedule to keep track of deadlines.

During the production stage, we would use the layouts to create the 3D models and animate the scenes. We would also create a list of props and work on the music score. A budget chart would be used to keep track of expenses, and we would obtain release forms from talent and locations.

In conclusion, production planning is crucial to the success of a 2D or 3D film. By using charts and elements such as storyboards, animatics, layouts, shot progress charts, global shot schedules, props, music, budgets, and release forms, we can effectively plan and execute a film project.

ACTOR RELEASE FORM

I, [Actor Name], hereby grant full and exclusive rights to the Executive Producer of the film [Film Title], to use, reuse, publish, and republish any and all audio and/or visual recordings of my performance in said film, without limitation or restriction.

I hereby acknowledge and agree that the Executive Producer owns all right, title, and interest in and to the film, and that my participation in the film shall not entitle me to any ownership or financial interest in said film.

I agree to release the Executive Producer, its agents, employees, and assigns from any and all claims, actions, demands, or suits that may arise in connection with the use of my performance in the film.

I warrant and represent that I have the right and authority to enter into this release and that my performance in the film does not violate any third-party rights or any applicable laws.

I have read and fully understand the terms of this release and voluntarily sign it with the understanding that it is binding upon me, my heirs, legal representatives, and assigns.

Actor Signature: _____

Print Name: _____

Date: _____

2D ANIMATIC

A 2D animatic is a pre-visualization tool used in animation and filmmaking to plan and storyboard the visual and timing aspects of an animated or live-action project. It is essentially a rough cut of the animation or film, with still images or simple motion graphics set to sound and dialogue.

The use of animatics in animation dates back to the early days of Walt Disney Studios in the 1930s, where they were used to plan out the timing and sequence of animated films. These early animatics were created using hand-drawn sketches and photographs, and were called "story reels" or "story sketches."

As animation technology evolved, animatics moved into the digital realm. In the 1990s, computer-generated 3D animatics became popular in Hollywood as a way to pre-visualize and plan complex visual effects and action sequences in films. 2D animatics continued to be used for more traditional 2D animation projects.

Today, 2D animatics are commonly used in animation and filmmaking as a way to communicate the pacing, timing, and visual style of a project to directors, producers, and animators. They are also used to help secure funding for projects and to test story concepts before moving on to full production.

The exact history of who created the first 2D animatic is unclear, as it is an evolution of traditional storyboards and early animatics. However, it is generally credited to the animation industry as a whole and its ongoing effort to find ways to plan, visualize and refine animation projects before committing to the full animation process.

Creating a 2D animatic involves a series of steps that help to visualize the story, sequence, and timing of your animation project. Here are the general directions on how to create a 2D animatic:

Step 1: Develop a Storyboard - Before creating an animatic, it's important to have a visual plan for the animation. You can create a storyboard by drawing a series of sketches that depict the main events and actions of your story. You can also add notes on the dialogue, sound effects, and camera angles.

Step 2: Assemble the Shots - Once you have the storyboard, scan or photograph each panel and import them into a software program such as Adobe Photoshop or Adobe Illustrator. Organize the shots in the order of the storyboard and arrange them on a timeline.

Step 3: Add Timing and Sound - An animatic is essentially a rough cut of the animation, so it's important to add timing and sound to help communicate the pacing of the story. You can add a timecode to each shot to indicate the duration, and also add sound effects and dialogue using a separate audio track.

Step 4: Refine and Edit - Once you have assembled the shots, timing, and sound, it's time to refine and edit the animatic. You can adjust the timing of the shots, add or remove frames, and make any necessary changes to the dialogue or sound effects. You can also add camera movements and zooms to enhance the visual storytelling.

Step 5: Finalize and Export - Once you are satisfied with the animatic, it's time to export it into a video file format. You can choose to export it as a QuickTime movie, MP4, or other formats depending on your preference. You can also add a title card at the beginning and end of the animatic to indicate the title, creator, and other relevant information.

Overall, creating a 2D animatic requires careful planning, attention to detail, and good storytelling skills. By following these directions, you can create a rough cut of your animation project that helps you visualize the story and timing before moving on to the final production phase.

3D ANIMATIC

A 3D animatic, similar to a 2D animatic, is a pre-visualization tool used in animation and filmmaking to plan and storyboard the visual and timing aspects of an animated or live-action project. However, instead of using still images or simple motion graphics, a 3D animatic is a rough cut of the animation or film created using 3D models and computer animation software.

The use of 3D animatics became popular in Hollywood in the 1990s as a way to pre-visualize and plan complex visual effects and action sequences in films. The 3D models allowed for more precise camera angles and movements, as well as the ability to incorporate lighting and textures.

The creation of 3D animatics was made possible by advancements in computer animation software, including the development of Autodesk Maya, which is still widely used in the industry today. The use of 3D animatics continues to be an important tool in modern filmmaking, allowing directors and animators to plan and refine projects before moving on to full production.

The exact history of who created the first 3D animatic is unclear, as it is an evolution of traditional storyboards and early animatics. However, it is generally credited to the animation industry as a whole and its ongoing effort to find ways to plan, visualize and refine animation projects before committing to the full animation process.

LOCATION RELEASE

[Production Company Logo]

Location Release Form

Property Owner's Name:

Property Address:

_____

In consideration for the sum of $_____, receipt of which is hereby acknowledged, I, the undersigned property owner, hereby grant permission to [Production Company Name] ("Production Company") and its representatives to enter the above-listed property on _____ (date) and to use the property in connection with the production of a motion picture tentatively entitled "[Film Title]" (the "Film").

I represent and warrant that I am the owner or authorized agent of the owner of the property, and have the full right, power, and authority to execute this release.

I understand and agree that the Production Company has the right to use the property, including any buildings or structures on the property, for the purpose of filming, photography, and sound recording in connection with the Film. I hereby grant the Production Company and its representatives the right to use my property and its contents, fixtures, equipment, furniture, and other items that may be visible or audible on camera or microphone.

I acknowledge and agree that the Production Company shall have the right to edit, alter, and/or use the footage taken on the property in any manner it deems appropriate in connection with the Film, without any obligation to me, my heirs, assigns, or successors.

I hereby release and discharge the Production Company, its employees, agents, officers, and directors, from any and all claims, demands, actions, or causes of action that I may have for libel, slander, invasion of privacy, or any other cause arising out of the Production Company's use of the property or any of the items located thereon.

I understand that the Production Company will be solely responsible for any damage that may occur to the property as a result of its use in connection with the Film.

This release shall be binding upon me, my heirs, assigns, and successors. This release represents the entire understanding between the parties and supersedes all prior negotiations and understandings.

Signed:

Property Owner

Date: _____

Witness:

Date: _____

INVOKING COLOR IN FILM AND EDITING TECHNIQUES

Coloring in film is the process of enhancing the visual appearance of a film through the use of color grading. This involves adjusting the color balance, saturation, contrast, and brightness of the footage to create a specific mood or atmosphere. Different colors can be used to evoke different emotions and convey different meanings. Here are some examples of how colors can be used in film:

Red: This color is often associated with passion, danger, and anger. It can be used to create a sense of tension or urgency. For example, in the film "The Shining," the color red is used to signify the presence of danger and violence.

Purple: This color is often associated with mystery, royalty, and spirituality. It can be used to create a sense of otherworldliness or fantasy. For example, in the film "Avatar," the color purple is used to signify the spiritual connection between the Na'vi and their environment.

Orange: This color is often associated with warmth, energy, and excitement. It can be used to create a sense of enthusiasm or vitality. For example, in the film "Whiplash," the color orange is used to signify the intensity and passion of the jazz music being played.

Yellow: This color is often associated with happiness, optimism, and enlightenment. It can be used to create a sense of joy or positivity. For example, in the film "La La Land," the color yellow is used to signify the hopeful and optimistic tone of the story.

Cutting points in film refer to the moments when a new shot or scene is introduced. These cutting points can be used to create a variety of effects and can be based on different factors, such as shape, color, motion, or sound. Here are some examples of different cutting points and their pros and cons:

Cutting on a shape: This technique involves cutting from one shot to another based on a similar shape or pattern. This can create a sense of continuity and can be used to emphasize a particular visual element. However, it can also be repetitive and can become distracting if overused.

Cutting on a color: This technique involves cutting from one shot to another based on a similar color or tone. This can create a sense of unity and can be used to highlight a particular mood or emotion. However, it can also be monotonous and can limit the visual variety of the film.

Cutting on motion: This technique involves cutting from one shot to another based on a similar movement or action. This can create a sense of flow and can be used to emphasize a particular action or activity. However, it can also be disorienting and can disrupt the continuity of the film if used incorrectly.

J cut: This technique involves introducing the audio from the next scene before the corresponding visual element is shown. This can create a sense of anticipation and can be used to smoothly transition between scenes. However, it can also be confusing and can interrupt the rhythm of the film if used improperly.

L cut: This technique involves allowing the audio from the previous scene to continue into the next scene before it is shown visually. This can create a sense of continuity and can be used to establish a particular mood or tone. However, it can also be repetitive and can become tedious if overused.

Overall, the use of cutting points in film can greatly impact the overall feel and pacing of the film. It's important to consider the pros and cons of each technique and to use them appropriately to enhance the story being told.

WHAT IS DAZ STUDIOS STUDIOS

DAZ STUDIOS

Daz Studio is a 3D software application that enables users to create and animate 3D models, characters, and scenes. It is designed to be user-friendly and flexible, allowing users to create 3D content quickly and easily, without requiring extensive technical knowledge.

Daz Studio is capable of creating high-quality 3D content for use in various applications, such as film, animation, and gaming. Its capabilities include 3D modeling, rigging, animation, texturing, rendering, and more. The software also comes with a large library of pre-built 3D models, poses, and environments that users can utilize in their projects.

To download and install Daz Studio, follow these steps:

Go to the Daz Studio website: https://www.daz3d.com/get_studio

Click on the "Download Now" button for the version of Daz Studio you want to install (Windows or Mac).

Once the download is complete, run the installation file and follow the on-screen instructions.

System Requirements for Daz Studio on Windows:

Windows 10 64-bit

3GHz+ quad-core processor

8GB+ RAM

OpenGL 4.0 compatible graphics card with 2GB+ RAM

1GB+ free hard drive space

System Requirements for Daz Studio on Mac OS X:

macOS 10.14 or later

3GHz+ quad-core processor

8GB+ RAM

OpenGL 4.0 compatible graphics card with 2GB+ RAM

1GB+ free hard drive space

To import an OBJ or FBX file in Daz Studio, follow these steps:

Open Daz Studio and select "File" > "Import" > "Wavefront OBJ" or "Autodesk FBX", depending on the file format you have.

Browse to the location of the file you want to import and select it.

In the import options dialog box, adjust any settings as necessary, such as scaling or texture mapping.

Click "Accept" to import the file.

To create an environment in Daz Studio, follow these steps:

Click on the "Environment" tab in the top menu bar.

Select "Create New Environment".

Choose the type of environment you want to create, such as an outdoor scene or a room.

Use the tools provided to customize the environment, such as adding objects, adjusting lighting, and changing the camera view.

Save your environment as a preset for future use.

To render out a shot in Daz Studio, follow these steps:

Set up your scene with the objects, characters, and environment you want to render.

Choose your camera view and adjust it as necessary.

Click on the "Render" tab in the top menu bar.

Adjust any render settings, such as resolution, lighting, and effects.

Click "Render" to begin the rendering process.

Once rendering is complete, save your rendered image or animation to your desired location.

CREATING CHARACTERS & TIMELINE

To create a Genesis 8 or 9 character in Daz Studio, follow these steps:

Open Daz Studio and select "Create" > "New Figure" from the top menu.

Choose "Genesis 8 Female" or "Genesis 8 Male" from the list of available figures.

Customize your character by selecting the various options available, such as skin tone, eye color, hairstyle, clothing, and accessories.

Use the morph dials to adjust the character's body shape, facial features, and other attributes.

Save your character as a preset for future use.

To create a camera in Daz Studio, follow these steps:

Click on the "Camera" tab in the top menu bar.

Select "Create New Camera" from the dropdown menu.

Choose the type of camera you want to create, such as a perspective camera or an orthographic camera.

Use the tools provided to adjust the camera's position, rotation, and focal length.

Save your camera as a preset for future use.

To animate a camera in Daz Studio, follow these steps:

Create a camera as described above.

Switch to the "Timeline" tab in the top menu bar.

Select the camera you want to animate from the list of available objects.

Move the timeline marker to the point where you want the animation to start.

Use the camera tools to adjust the camera's position, rotation, and focal length.

Click on the "Set Keyframe" button to add a keyframe for the camera at the current time.

Move the timeline marker to the point where you want the animation to end.

Use the camera tools to adjust the camera's position, rotation, and focal length again.

Click on the "Set Keyframe" button to add a keyframe for the camera at the end time.

Preview your animation by scrubbing through the timeline.

The timeline in Daz Studio is used to control the timing of animations. Keyframes are used to mark specific points in time where an object's position, rotation, or other properties change. To create a keyframe, select the object you want to animate, move the timeline marker to the desired point in time, and then adjust the object's properties as desired. Click the "Set Keyframe" button to add a keyframe at the current time. You can then move the timeline marker and adjust the object's properties again to create additional keyframes.

To add lighting to an environment in Daz Studio, follow these steps:

Click on the "Render Settings" tab in the top menu bar.

Select "Environment" from the list of available settings.

Click on the "Add" button to add a new environment setting.

Choose the type of lighting you want to use, such as an IBL (image-based lighting) or a mesh light.

Use the tools provided to adjust the lighting's position, intensity, and color.

Preview your lighting by rendering a test shot.

IBL lighting uses a high-resolution image to provide realistic lighting for your scene. To use IBL lighting in Daz Studio, select the IBL option and choose an image from your computer or from the Daz Studio library. Mesh lights are 3D objects that emit light, and can be positioned and adjusted like any other object in your scene.

LIGHTS AND CAMERAS IN DAZ STUDIO

Daz Studio offers a variety of lights and cameras, as well as options for adjusting focal lengths and rendering settings, to give you greater control over your scenes and animations.

Lights:

Daz Studio offers several types of lights, including point lights, spotlights, and distant lights.

Point lights emit light equally in all directions from a single point in space. They are useful for creating soft, ambient lighting.

Spotlights emit light in a cone shape, allowing you to direct the light precisely where you want it. They are useful for creating dramatic lighting effects.

Distant lights act like a sun or moon, emitting light from a single direction. They are useful for creating realistic outdoor lighting.

Cameras:

Daz Studio offers several types of cameras, including perspective cameras, orthographic cameras, and panoramic cameras.

Perspective cameras mimic the way the human eye sees, creating a sense of depth and dimension in your scenes.

Orthographic cameras do not have any perspective distortion, and are useful for creating technical illustrations or diagrams.

Panoramic cameras allow you to capture a 360-degree view of your scene, and are useful for creating immersive virtual reality experiences.

Focal lengths:

Daz Studio allows you to adjust the focal length of your camera, which affects the perspective and depth of field in your scene.

Short focal lengths (wide-angle lenses) create a wider field of view, making objects appear smaller and farther away.

Long focal lengths (telephoto lenses) create a narrower field of view, making objects appear larger and closer.

Rendering options:

Daz Studio offers a variety of rendering options to help you achieve the desired look for your scene or animation.

You can adjust the resolution, anti-aliasing, and other quality settings to balance rendering speed and image quality.

Daz Studio also offers options for rendering with Iray or 3Delight, which are different rendering engines with different strengths and weaknesses.

Additionally, you can choose to render your scene as a still image or as an animation, and select the file format and other output settings as desired.

HOW TO APPLY SKIN COLOR AND LOADING CHARACTER GENESIS 8 OR 9

How to apply texture and skin color to a character in Daz Studio:

Open Daz Studio and load a Genesis 8 or 9 character.

Go to the Surfaces tab and select the body part you want to apply the texture to.

Click on the Base Color option and select the texture you want to apply from the Content Library.

Adjust the Scale and Offset settings to fine-tune the placement of the texture on the character.

Repeat the process for each body part you want to apply a texture to.

To apply skin color, go to the Base Color option for the character's skin.

Choose a base skin tone from the preset options, or create a custom skin tone by adjusting the Hue, Saturation, and Value sliders.

Use the Glossy Layered Weight option to adjust the shininess of the skin.

Use the Subsurface Color option to adjust the color of light that passes through the skin.

Use the Subsurface Radius option to adjust the amount of light scattering beneath the skin.

Adjust the other options in the Surfaces tab as desired to fine-tune the character's appearance.

To apply a face generator, go to the Shaping tab and select the Face option.

Choose a preset face shape or create a custom face shape by adjusting the sliders for each feature.

Use the Head Morphs option to adjust the overall shape of the head and face.

Use the Face Details option to adjust the finer details of the face, such as wrinkles and blemishes.

Use the Expression Presets option to add emotions and facial expressions to the character.

Adjust the other options in the Shaping tab as desired to fine-tune the character's facial features.

To add hair and clothing to the character, go to the Hair and Wardrobe tabs and select the desired options.

Use the Camera and Lights tabs to adjust the scene lighting and camera angle as desired.

When you are satisfied with the scene, go to the Render tab and select the desired rendering options. Click the Render button to render the scene.

How to create a scene for virtual film in Daz Studio (detailed steps from 1-20):

Open Daz Studio and go to the Content Library.

Choose a background or environment from the Scenes folder and load it into the viewport.

Load a Genesis 8 or 9 character into the scene.

Use the instructions above to apply textures and skin color to the character, and to create a custom face shape using the Face generator.

Choose hair and clothing options for the character from the Hair and Wardrobe tabs.

Use the Camera tab to adjust the camera angle and position as desired.

Use the Lights tab to add and adjust lights in the scene.

Use the Surfaces tab to adjust the materials and textures of the environment, such as the floor or walls.

Add props to the scene, such as furniture or other objects, from the Content Library.

Use the Timeline tab to create keyframes for the character's movements and actions.

Move the character into position for the first shot and create a keyframe.

Move the character to the next position for the second shot and create another keyframe.

Continue adding keyframes and moving the character until the animation is complete.

Use the Graph Editor to adjust the timing and easing of the keyframes for a smoother animation.

Use the Render Settings tab to adjust the quality and output settings for the animation.

Preview the animation in the Preview window to ensure that it looks as desired.

When you are satisfied with the animation, click

IMPORTING 3D AND IMPORT MUSIC MP3

Instructions for importing 3D object and FBX in Daz Studio:

Open Daz Studio and go to the File menu.

Click on the Import option and choose the 3D object or FBX file you want to import.

Click on the Options button to adjust the import settings, such as the scale and orientation of the object.

Click on the Import button to import the object into the scene.

Instructions for rendering a PNG or MP4/MOV file from Daz Studio:

Load the scene you want to render in Daz Studio.

Go to the Render Settings tab and adjust the render settings as desired, such as the resolution and quality.

Choose the output format you want to render to, such as PNG or MP4/MOV.

Click on the Render button to begin the rendering process.

When the rendering is complete, go to the Render folder in the Content Library to find your rendered files.

Instructions for importing sound MP3, AVI, AAC file in Daz Studio:

Open Daz Studio and load the scene you want to add sound to.

Go to the Timeline tab and click on the Audio button to add an audio track.

Click on the Import Audio button and choose the sound file you want to import, such as an MP3, AVI, or AAC file.

Use the drag handles on the audio track to adjust the start and end times of the sound.

Use the volume slider to adjust the volume of the sound.

Preview the scene to ensure that the sound is playing correctly.

Mixamo is a web-based service that allows users to create, customize, and download 3D character models and animations. In order to use Mixamo, users must first create an account on the website.

System Requirements:

For Mac OSX:

OS X 10.9 or higher

Safari 7 or higher

Google Chrome

For Windows:

Windows 7 or higher

Google Chrome

Firefox

Instructions for Downloading Mixamo:

Open a web browser and go to mixamo.com.

Click on the "Get Started for Free" button located in the top right corner of the homepage.

Enter your email address and create a password to create an account.

Once logged in, click on the "Characters" tab in the navigation menu at the top of the page.

Choose a character that you would like to download by clicking on the thumbnail.

Customize the character by choosing different options such as clothing, hairstyle, and accessories.

Once you are satisfied with your character, click on the "Download" button located in the bottom right corner of the screen.

Choose the desired file format and click on the "Download" button again.

The file will then download to your computer.

The purpose of Mixamo is to provide users with an easy and efficient way to create and download high-quality 3D character models and animations for use in various projects, such as video games, movies, and animations.

Interface and How to Use It:

The Mixamo interface is user-friendly and intuitive. When you first log in, you will see a navigation menu at the top of the screen that allows you to access various features, such as characters, animations, and account settings.

To import a character, follow these steps:

Click on the "Characters" tab in the navigation menu.

Choose a character that you would like to import by clicking on the thumbnail.

Customize the character by choosing different options such as clothing, hairstyle, and accessories.

Once you are satisfied with your character, click on the "Download" button located in the bottom right corner of the screen.

Choose the desired file format and click on the "Download" button again.

The file will then download to your computer.

To export a character, follow these steps:

Click on the "Characters" tab in the navigation menu.

Choose a character that you would like to export by clicking on the thumbnail.

Click on the "Export" button located in the bottom left corner of the screen.

Choose the desired file format and click on the "Download" button.

The file will then download to your computer.

Mixamo offers a wide range of animations and characters that are built into the software. As of September 2021, there are over 7,000 character models and over 11,000 animations available on the website. These include both free and paid options, with many different styles and genres to choose from.

UNREAL ENGINE WHAT DOES IT DO WHERE DID IT COME FROM

Unreal Engine is a powerful game engine developed by Epic Games that is used for creating video games, simulations, and other interactive experiences. Here are the instructions for downloading Unreal Engine and using it to import and export characters:

System Requirements:

For Mac OSX:

macOS 10.14 or later

Quad-core Intel or AMD processor, 2.5 GHz or faster

NVIDIA GeForce 470 GTX or AMD Radeon 6870 HD series card or higher

8 GB RAM

5 GB of free hard drive space

For Windows:

Windows 10 64-bit

Quad-core Intel or AMD processor, 2.5 GHz or faster

NVIDIA GeForce 470 GTX or AMD Radeon 6870 HD series card or higher

8 GB RAM

5 GB of free hard drive space

Instructions for Downloading Unreal Engine:

Go to unrealengine.com and click on "Get Started" at the top of the page.

Create an account or sign in with an existing account.

Download the Epic Games Launcher and install it on your computer.

Open the Epic Games Launcher and click on the "Unreal Engine" tab on the left-hand side.

Click on the "Install" button and select the version of Unreal Engine that you would like to download.

Once the installation is complete, click on the "Launch" button to open the Unreal Editor.

The purpose of Unreal Engine is to provide a powerful and versatile platform for creating high-quality interactive experiences, including video games, virtual reality simulations, and architectural visualizations.

Interface and How to Use It:

The Unreal Engine interface is divided into several panels, including the Content Browser, the World Outliner, and the Details panel. These panels allow you to manage assets, organize your scene, and adjust various properties of your objects.

To import a character, follow these steps:

In the Content Browser, click on the "Import" button and select the character file that you would like to import.

Choose the appropriate import settings, such as the scale and animation options.

Click on the "Import" button to import the character into your scene.

To export a character, follow these steps:

Select the character that you would like to export in the Content Browser or World Outliner.

Right-click on the selection and choose "Export" from the context menu.

Choose the desired export settings, such as the file format and export location.

Click on the "Export" button to export the character.

Unreal Engine comes with a number of built-in characters and animations, including a range of humanoid and non-humanoid characters. Additionally, Unreal Engine works seamlessly with other Epic Games products, such as the MetaHuman Creator, Quixel Megascans, and the Quixel Bridge.

The MetaHuman Creator is a cloud-based tool that allows you to create highly realistic human characters with a range of facial expressions and animations. To import a MetaHuman character into your Unreal Engine scene, follow these steps:

Create a MetaHuman character in the MetaHuman Creator.

Export the character to Unreal Engine using the "Export to Engine" button.

Open Unreal Engine and import the character using the Content Browser.

Quixel Megascans is a library of high-quality 3D assets, including textures, models, and materials. To use Megascans assets in Unreal Engine, you can use the Quixel Bridge tool to download and import the assets directly into your Unreal Engine project. To import a Megascans asset into your scene, follow these steps:

Install and open the Quixel Bridge tool.

Browse the Megascans library and select the asset that you would like to use.

VERSION RELEASE OF UNREAL ENGINE

Unreal Engine is regularly updated with new features and improvements. Here's an overview of the different versions of Unreal Engine, along with their pros and cons:

Unreal Engine 5: The latest version of Unreal Engine, released in 2021. It includes new features such as Nanite (a geometry system that allows for detailed scenes with billions of polygons), Lumen (a global illumination system), and MetaHuman Creator (a cloud-based tool for creating realistic human characters). Pros: Improved graphics and performance, new tools for creating realistic characters and environments. Cons: Some features are still in development, may require more powerful hardware to run.

Unreal Engine 4: The previous version of Unreal Engine, released in 2014. It includes features such as Blueprints (a visual scripting system), Cascade (a particle system), and Sequencer (a cinematic editing tool). Pros: Stable and mature, widely used in the game development industry, extensive documentation and community support. Cons: May not have the latest features and improvements.

Unreal Engine 3: The previous previous version of Unreal Engine, released in 2006. It was used to create many popular games from the mid-2000s to early 2010s. Pros: Widely used and well-established, good performance on older hardware. Cons: Outdated compared to newer versions, limited support and documentation.

To change the direction of a directional light in Unreal Engine, follow these steps:

In the World Outliner, select the directional light that you want to adjust.

In the Details panel, find the "Rotation" property under "Transform" and adjust the values to change the direction of the light.

Volumetric clouds and HDR backgrounds can add realism and atmosphere to your Unreal Engine scene. To import and use them, follow these steps:

Find a suitable volumetric cloud or HDR background asset, either from the Unreal Engine Marketplace or from a third-party source.

Import the asset into your project using the Content Browser.

In the Level Editor, drag the asset into your scene and adjust the properties to fit your needs.

To render a sequence or camera from Unreal Engine, follow these steps:

In the Level Editor, open the "Sequencer" tool.

Create a new sequence or open an existing one.

Add cameras and other objects to your sequence as desired.

Use the "Render Movie" button to export your sequence or camera to a video file.

To import an FBX file or Mixamo animation into Unreal Engine, follow these steps:

In the Content Browser, click on the "Import" button and select the FBX file or Mixamo animation that you want to import.

Choose the appropriate import settings, such as the scale and animation options.

Click on the "Import" button to import the asset into your project.

To import a camera track from After Effects into Unreal Engine, follow these steps:

Export your After Effects project as an FBX file.

In Unreal Engine, use the Content Browser to import the FBX file.

In the Level Editor, select the imported camera object and adjust the properties as desired.

When creating visuals for a film, Unreal Engine can be used for a wide range of tasks, including:

Previsualization: Creating rough drafts of scenes to plan camera angles, lighting, and other details.

Virtual production: Using real-time rendering and motion capture to create realistic sets and characters on a budget.

Post-production: Adding special effects, compositing, and other finishing touches to footage using Unreal Engine's built-in tools.

Interactive experiences: Creating immersive experiences for audiences using VR or other interactive technologies.

CREATING PHOTOREAL VIDEO IN UNREAL ENGINE

First, create a new project in Unreal Engine and choose the appropriate template for your scene (e.g. architectural visualization, product showcase, etc.).

Use the Content Browser to import any assets that you want to use in your scene, such as 3D models, textures, and materials.

Place the assets in the Level Editor and arrange them to create your desired scene.

Use the Material Editor to create realistic materials for your assets, using textures and other settings to achieve the desired look.

Use the Lightmass settings to adjust the lighting in your scene, including the intensity, color, and direction of lights.

Use the Post Process Volume to adjust the overall look of your scene, including color grading, bloom, and other effects.

Use the Camera settings to adjust the camera angle and field of view for your scene.

Use the Sequencer tool to create a cinematic sequence for your scene, including camera movements, animations, and sound effects.

Use the Matinee tool to create scripted events for your scene, such as triggered animations or special effects.

Use the Blueprint tool to create interactive elements for your scene, such as buttons or switches.

Use the Physics tool to create realistic interactions between objects in your scene, such as collision and gravity.

Use the Audio tool to add sound effects and music to your scene.

Use the Level Blueprint to create scripted events that affect the entire level, such as changing the time of day or activating a weather system.

Use the Game Mode Blueprint to create custom game mechanics for your scene, such as puzzles or objectives.

Use the VR tool to create immersive virtual reality experiences for your scene.

Use the Crowd tool to create realistic crowds of people or other creatures in your scene.

Use the Landscape tool to create realistic outdoor environments for your scene, including terrain, foliage, and water.

Use the Substance tool to create realistic procedural textures for your scene, such as rust or grime.

Use the Datasmith tool to import data from other 3D modeling programs, such as Autodesk Maya or 3ds Max.

Finally, use the Sequencer tool to render a high-quality video of your scene.

To edit a scene using timeline and keyframing in Unreal Engine:

Open your project in Unreal Engine and select the Sequencer tool.

In the Sequencer, select the camera or object that you want to animate.

Set the keyframes for the object's position, rotation, or other properties.

Use the timeline to adjust the timing of the animation and add additional keyframes as needed.

Preview the animation in the Sequencer and make any necessary adjustments.

Render the animation using the "Render Movie" button.

To connect Bridge and create a MetaHuman step by step to use in Unreal Engine:

Download and install Quixel Bridge.

Launch Bridge and sign in to your Quixel account.

Select the "MetaHumans" tab in Bridge and choose a MetaHuman character that you want to use.

Customize the character's appearance using the built-in controls, such as changing the hairstyle or clothing.

Export the character as an FBX file.

Open Unreal Engine and create a new project.

Use the Content Browser to import the FBX file.

Add the character to your scene and adjust its position and scale as needed.

Use the Material Editor to customize the character's materials and textures.

Use the Sequencer or Matinee tool to animate the character's movements and interactions with other objects in the scene.

QUIXEL BRIDGE

What is Quixel bridge

Quixel Bridge is a tool that allows artists and designers to easily browse and download thousands of high-quality 3D assets and materials from the Quixel Megascans library, as well as create and customize MetaHuman characters for use in Unreal Engine.

To use Quixel Bridge with Megascans environments and MetaHuman characters in Unreal Engine:

Download and install Quixel Bridge.

Launch Bridge and sign in to your Quixel account.

Browse the Megascans library and select the assets that you want to use in your Unreal Engine project.

Customize the assets using the built-in controls, such as adjusting the texture resolution or adding procedural variation.

Export the assets as FBX files.

Open Unreal Engine and create a new project.

Use the Content Browser to import the FBX files.

Place the assets in the Level Editor and arrange them to create your desired scene.

Use the Material Editor to create realistic materials for your assets, using textures and other settings to achieve the desired look.

Use the Post Process Volume to adjust the overall look of your scene, including color grading, bloom, and other effects.

Use the Level Blueprint to create scripted events that affect the entire level, such as changing the time of day or activating a weather system.

Use the Sequencer tool to create a cinematic sequence for your scene, including camera movements, animations, and sound effects.

Use the MetaHuman Creator tool to create and customize realistic human characters for use in your scene.

The Unreal Engine Sequencer is a powerful tool for creating cinematic sequences and animations within the engine. It allows users to create complex camera movements, add sound effects and music, and incorporate animations and special effects. The Sequencer also supports keyframing and timeline-based editing, allowing users to precisely control the timing and pacing of their sequences.

The Level Blueprint is a visual scripting tool that allows users to create interactive gameplay mechanics and scripted events within a level. It provides a graphical interface for creating and connecting events, conditions, and actions, making it easier for non-programmers to create custom gameplay experiences.

The Post Process Volume is a tool that allows users to adjust the overall look of a scene, including color grading, bloom, and other effects. By adding a Post Process Volume to a scene, users can quickly and easily adjust the tone and mood of their environment, making it easier to create a photorealistic or stylized look.

The Material Editor is a tool that allows users to create and edit materials for objects and surfaces within a scene. It provides a node-based interface for connecting textures, parameters, and other settings, allowing users to create complex, realistic materials that respond dynamically to changes in lighting and other factors. The Material Editor is a powerful tool for creating photorealistic or stylized visuals within Unreal Engine.

CREATING A FIRST-PERSON SHOOTER GAME IN UNREAL ENGINE

Creating a first-person shooter and basic maze puzzle video game with Unreal Engine is a fun and exciting project that can be accomplished with the help of the Level Blueprint and MetaHumans. Here are some instructions to get started:

Launch Unreal Engine and create a new project.

Add a new level to the project and name it "Maze Level."

Use the geometry tools to create a maze inside the level.

Add a First Person Character to the level and position it at the start of the maze.

Add a Trigger Box to the level and position it at the end of the maze.

Open the Level Blueprint and create a new event for when the player enters the Trigger Box.

Inside the event, add a node to play a sound effect and display a message to the player that they have completed the maze.

Add a new Blueprint class for a gun and create a shooting mechanic for the First Person Character.

Create enemies in the form of MetaHumans and add them to the maze.

Add AI behavior to the MetaHumans so that they will attack the player on sight.

Create a health system for the player and the enemies.

Add pickups for health and ammo throughout the maze.

Create a timer for the game and add a node to end the game when the time runs out.

Add a menu system for the start and end of the game.

Playtest the game and make adjustments as necessary.

Keyframing and timeline-based editing are important tools in Unreal Engine for creating cinematic sequences and animations. Keyframing involves setting keyframes for different elements of a scene or animation, and then adjusting those elements over time to create movement or change. Timeline-based editing allows users to adjust the timing and pacing of those keyframes to create a specific effect or sequence.

To use keyframing and timeline-based editing in Unreal Engine:

Open the Sequencer tool.

Create a new sequence for the animation or sequence you want to create.

Add actors to the sequence, including MetaHumans or other objects in the scene.

Set keyframes for different properties of those actors, such as position, rotation, or scale.

Use the timeline to adjust the timing and pacing of those keyframes, creating the desired effect or sequence.

Add audio, visual effects, and other elements to enhance the sequence.

Preview the sequence in real-time to make adjustments as necessary.

Render the sequence for use in the final game or project.

Using keyframing and timeline-based editing in Unreal Engine can create engaging and dynamic sequences that enhance the gameplay and overall experience of a video game.

WHAT ARE METAHUMANS

MetaHumans is a software by Epic Games that allows users to create realistic human characters with advanced facial and body animations for use in video games, films, and other digital media. Here's how to download the software and use it to create a MetaHuman:

Go to the MetaHuman Creator website at https://www.unrealengine.com/en-US/metahuman-creator.

Sign in with your Epic Games account or create a new account if you don't have one.

Click on the "Create a MetaHuman" button.

Choose the type of character you want to create, such as male or female, and select the base template that fits your vision.

Use the controls on the left side of the screen to adjust the character's features, including hair, skin tone, and facial expressions.

Use the controls on the right side of the screen to adjust the character's body shape and size.

Use the animation tools to create custom animations for your MetaHuman, or choose from pre-built animations to add to your character.

Preview and adjust your character until you are satisfied with the results.

Download your MetaHuman as an FBX file to use in Unreal Engine or Mixamo.

Here's a lesson and exercise on how to create and add animation and import a MetaHuman into Unreal Engine or Mixamo:

Lesson: Creating and Animating a MetaHuman

In this lesson, you will learn how to create and animate a MetaHuman using the MetaHuman Creator software and import it into Unreal Engine or Mixamo.

Exercise:

Open the MetaHuman Creator website and create a new MetaHuman.

Customize the character's features and body to fit your vision.

Use the animation tools to create a custom animation for your MetaHuman, such as a walking or running animation.

Download your MetaHuman as an FBX file.

Open Unreal Engine or Mixamo and import your MetaHuman.

Use the animation tools in Unreal Engine or Mixamo to add additional animations to your MetaHuman, such as jumping or shooting animations.

Use the Level Blueprint and other tools in Unreal Engine to create a game environment for your MetaHuman.

Playtest your game and make adjustments as necessary.

Export your game as a standalone executable or publish it on a game platform.

By following these steps, you can create and animate a MetaHuman character and import it into Unreal Engine or Mixamo for use in a video game or other digital media project.

The differences between unreal engine, Daz studios, mixamo.com, and meta-human creator as well as Autodesk Maya and aftereffects discuss the pros and cons and which application is the best rate for combining CGI and live-action footage

Unreal Engine, Daz Studio, Mixamo.com, MetaHuman Creator, Autodesk Maya, and AfterEffects are all software applications used for creating CGI and combining it with live-action footage. Each application has its pros and cons, and the best one to use depends on the specific project's requirements.

Unreal Engine is a game engine used for creating interactive experiences, including video games and virtual reality applications. It has a powerful rendering engine, supports real-time rendering, and includes a robust toolset for creating game environments and characters. Unreal Engine is suitable for creating complex, large-scale projects that require a high degree of interactivity.

Daz Studio is a 3D modeling software designed for creating 3D figures and digital art. It includes a large library of pre-built characters, props, and environments, making it ideal for artists who want to create high-quality 3D content without spending a lot of time on modeling and texturing.

Mixamo.com is a web-based platform for creating 3D characters and animations. It includes a large library of pre-built characters and animations that can be customized using a simple interface. Mixamo is ideal for creating simple 3D characters and animations quickly and easily.

MetaHuman Creator is a software by Epic Games that allows users to create realistic human characters with advanced facial and body animations for use in video games, films, and other digital media. It includes a powerful animation toolset and a wide range of pre-built animations, making it ideal for creating realistic human characters quickly and easily.

Autodesk Maya is a 3D animation software used for creating complex, high-quality 3D models, animations, and visual effects. It includes a powerful toolset for modeling, texturing, and animating 3D characters and environments, making it suitable for creating high-quality CGI for films, video games, and other digital media.

AfterEffects is a compositing software used for creating visual effects and motion graphics. It includes a powerful toolset for combining live-action footage with CGI elements, making it ideal for creating complex visual effects sequences for films and other digital media.

In terms of combining CGI with live-action footage, the best software to use depends on the specific project's requirements. Unreal Engine and Maya are suitable for creating complex, high-quality 3D models and environments, while Daz Studio and Mixamo are ideal for creating simple 3D characters and animations quickly and easily. AfterEffects is suitable for compositing live-action footage with CGI elements, while MetaHuman Creator is ideal for creating realistic human characters quickly and easily.

Manually importing and rigging a character from blender, turbo squid maya , mudbox or zbrush into mixamo and then give example how applying pre built animation to the character explain which menu items to select from interface dashboard

Manually importing and rigging a character from software such as Blender, TurboSquid Maya, Mudbox, or ZBrush into Mixamo can be a useful skill for creating custom characters and animations. Here's a step-by-step guide on how to do it:

Prepare your character: Before you can import your character into Mixamo, you'll need to prepare it. Make sure your character is rigged, and its mesh is optimized for animation. You can use software like Blender or Maya to rig and optimize your character.

Export your character: Once your character is ready, export it as an FBX file. Make sure to include the rig and the mesh in your export.

Import your character into Mixamo: Log in to Mixamo and click on the "Upload Character" button. Select your FBX file and wait for Mixamo to process it. Once the upload is complete, you'll see a preview of your character in the Mixamo viewer.

Rig your character: In the Mixamo viewer, you'll need to rig your character. Click on the "Rig" button to bring up the rigging options. Select the appropriate options for your character, such as the type of rig, the number of bones, and the skinning method.

Apply animations: Once your character is rigged, you can apply pre-built animations from the Mixamo library. Browse the library and select an animation that you want to apply to your character. Click on the "Download" button to download the animation as an FBX file.

Import the animation into your 3D software: After you've downloaded the animation, import it into your 3D software. Make sure to import it as an FBX file, and apply it to your character's rig.

Export your character with animation: Once you've applied the animation to your character, export it as an FBX file again. Make sure to include the animation in your export.

Import the character with animation back into Mixamo: Finally, import the FBX file back into Mixamo. You should now see your character with the applied animation in the Mixamo viewer.

To apply pre-built animations to your character in Mixamo, follow these steps:

Log in to Mixamo and click on the "Animations" tab.

Browse the animation library and select an animation that you want to apply to your character.

Click on the animation to preview it.

If you're happy with the animation, click on the "Download" button.

Select the file format that you want to download the animation in, such as FBX.

Once the download is complete, import the animation into your 3D software and apply it to your character's rig.

Export your character with animation as an FBX file.

Import the character with animation back into Mixamo.

In terms of selecting the appropriate menu items from the Mixamo interface dashboard, it will depend on the specific task you're trying to perform. However, in general, you'll need to use the "Upload Character" button to import your character, and the "Rig" button to rig it. To browse the animation library, you can use the "Animations" tab.

Adobe Aero what is is and how do you use it when you have and animated character from mixamo.com

Adobe Aero is an augmented reality authoring tool that allows you to create immersive experiences using digital content, such as 3D models, animations, and images. With Aero, you can build interactive AR scenes and bring them to life using your mobile device. You can also use Aero to import animated characters from Mixamo.com and integrate them into your AR scenes.

To use Aero with an animated character from Mixamo.com, follow these steps:

Download your animated character from Mixamo.com in FBX format.

Open Adobe Aero on your mobile device.

Click the "New Project" button to create a new project.

Select "Import" and choose the FBX file of your animated character.

Adjust the scale and position of the character as needed.

Add any additional 3D models or images to your scene as desired.

Use Aero's tools to animate your character and add interactivity to your scene.

Preview your scene in AR to test how it looks and feels in the real world.

Share your project with others or export it as a video or GIF.

By using Aero with your animated character from Mixamo.com, you can create unique and engaging AR experiences that are sure to captivate your audience.

THE THEORY OF MOTAGE IN FILM

Narrative:

Montage and B-roll are two essential techniques in filmmaking. Montage is a sequence of images or shots edited together to create a narrative or a visual effect, while B-roll refers to supplementary footage used to illustrate or support the main content. Both techniques are used to enhance the story, create a mood, or convey a message to the audience. In this class, we will explore the theory and practical application of creating montage and B-roll in filmmaking.

Instruction:

Introduction to Montage and B-roll

Explain the concept of montage and B-roll with examples from popular films such as Rocky, The Godfather, and Pulp Fiction.

Discuss the importance of these techniques in enhancing the story, creating a mood, or conveying a message to the audience.

Techniques of Montage Introduce the techniques of montage, such as parallel editing, jump cuts, and match cuts. Explain how these techniques can be used to create tension, establish a theme, or compress time.

Techniques of B-roll Introduce the techniques of B-roll, such as cutaway shots, establishing shots, and reaction shots. Explain how these techniques can be used to illustrate or support the main content, create a sense of place, or convey emotions.

Exercise: Creating Montage and B-roll Divide the class into small groups and assign each group a scene from a popular film. Instruct them to create a montage and B-roll sequence for the scene, using the techniques learned in class. Afterward, have each group present their sequence to the class and discuss how they used the techniques to enhance the story or create a mood.

Conclusion:

Review the key concepts learned in class, including the techniques of montage and B-roll.

Encourage the students to continue exploring these techniques in their own filmmaking projects.

References:

Rocky (1976) directed by John G. AvildsenThe Godfather (1972) directed by Francis Ford CoppolaPulp Fiction (1994) directed by Quentin Tarantino

WHAT IS LOGGING FOOTAGE AND HOW DO I EDIT A SCENE

Instruction for Class on Efficiently Logging Footage, Opening a Project, and Basic Editing for Teens and Young Adults:

Efficiently Logging Footage

Explain the importance of logging footage, which involves identifying and labeling clips before importing them into a video editing software.

Demonstrate how to create a naming convention for clips, such as using a combination of the location, date, and shot type.

Instruct the students to organize their clips into folders based on the shoot day or location.

Discuss the benefits of logging footage, such as saving time and preventing confusion during the editing process.

Opening a Project

Demonstrate how to open a new project in a video editing software, such as Adobe Premiere Pro or Final Cut Pro.

Explain the different options for project settings, such as the frame rate and resolution, and how they affect the final video.

Show how to import the logged footage into the project and organize it into bins or folders for easy access.
Basic Editing

Demonstrate how to create a new sequence, which is the timeline where the video will be edited.

Show how to add clips to the timeline by dragging and dropping them from the project panel.

Explain how to use the trim tool to adjust the in and out points of a clip and how to use the razor tool to split clips into smaller segments.

Show how to add transitions, such as cross-dissolves or fades, between clips to create a smooth flow.

Discuss the importance of audio in video editing and demonstrate how to adjust the volume levels or add music and sound effects.

Exercise: Editing a Short Video

Divide the class into small groups and assign each group a set of clips to edit into a short video.

Instruct them to use the techniques learned in class to log the footage, open a new project, and edit the clips into a coherent and engaging video.

Afterward, have each group present their video to the class and discuss the editing choices they made.

Conclusion

Review the key concepts learned in class, including efficiently logging footage, opening a project, and basic editing techniques.
Encourage the students to continue practicing their editing skills and to experiment with different techniques to create unique and compelling videos.

HOW TO EDIT A SCENE USING DA VINCI RESOLVE

Efficiently Logging Footage:

Efficiently logging footage is a crucial step in the video editing process. It involves identifying and labeling the clips before importing them into a video editing software. By doing so, it makes the editing process smoother and faster.

Create a naming convention: It is essential to create a naming convention for clips that are consistent and easy to understand. This can be done by using a combination of the location, date, and shot type. For example, "New York_Central Park_2023-05-01_Wide Shot."

Organize clips into folders: After naming the clips, it is essential to organize them into folders based on the shoot day or location. This helps to keep the footage organized and easily accessible during the editing process.

Opening a Project:

After logging the footage, the next step is to open a new project in a video editing software. Here are the steps to follow:

Choose a Video Editing Software: Choose a video editing software that suits your needs, such as Adobe Premiere Pro, Final Cut Pro, or DaVinci Resolve.

Select Project Settings: Select the appropriate project settings such as frame rate, resolution, and aspect ratio, depending on the requirements of your project.

Import Footage: Import the logged footage into the project and organize it into bins or folders for easy access.

Basic Editing:

Basic editing involves assembling the footage in the timeline and adjusting the clips to create a coherent and engaging video. Here are the basic steps to follow:

Create a New Sequence: Create a new sequence or timeline where the video will be edited. Select the appropriate settings such as frame rate and resolution.

Add Clips to the Timeline: Drag and drop the clips from the project panel to the timeline to add them to the sequence.

Use the Trim Tool: Use the trim tool to adjust the in and out points of a clip to create a smoother and more natural flow.

Use the Razor Tool: Use the razor tool to split clips into smaller segments and arrange them in the timeline.

Add Transitions: Add transitions, such as cross-dissolves or fades, between clips to create a smooth flow.

Audio Editing: Adjust the audio levels, add music or sound effects to enhance the video.

In conclusion, efficiently logging footage, opening a project, and basic editing are essential skills that are fundamental to video editing. It is important to create a naming convention for clips, organize them into folders, choose the appropriate project settings, and use basic editing techniques to create a coherent and engaging video. With practice and experimentation, these skills can be developed to create unique and compelling videos.

MONTAGES AND ITS DIFFRENCE ACCORING TO THE MOVIE GENRES

Montage is a technique used in film and video editing to create a sequence of shots that convey a particular idea or emotion. It involves the assembly of short clips or images into a longer sequence, often with the use of transitions, effects, and music. The resulting montage can be used to tell a story, evoke emotions, or highlight a theme.

The meaning of montage varies depending on the type of media it is used in. Here are some examples:

Montage in Music Videos: In music videos, montage is often used to create a visual narrative that complements the song's lyrics and melody. It can involve shots of the artist performing, scenic shots, or clips that illustrate the song's theme. The use of quick cuts, transitions, and effects can create a dynamic and engaging visual experience.

Montage in Short Films: In short films, montage can be used to condense time or depict a character's emotional state. It can involve a sequence of shots that show the passage of time or a character's thoughts or memories. The use of music, sound effects, and color grading can enhance the emotional impact of the montage.

Montage in Commercials: In commercials, montage is often used to convey a brand's message or highlight its product. It can involve shots of the product, happy customers, or lifestyle shots that show the product in use. The use of quick cuts, upbeat music, and bright colors can create a sense of excitement and appeal.

Montage in Genres: Montage can be used in various film and video genres, such as action, drama, or comedy. In action films, montage can be used to show the training or preparation of the protagonist. In dramas, montage can depict the emotional journey of the characters. In comedies, montage can create a humorous and fast-paced sequence of events.

In summary, montage is a versatile technique used in film and video editing to create a sequence of shots that convey a particular idea or emotion. Its meaning varies depending on the type of media it is used in, such as music videos, short films, commercials, or genres.

THE ART OF CREATIVE STORYING TELLING AND HOW TO GET THE AUDIENCE INVOLED.

Creative storytelling is the art of crafting a narrative that captivates and engages the audience, leaving a lasting impact on them. As a storyteller, it is essential to have the ability to evoke emotions and create a connection between the audience and the story. To be a better storyteller, here are some tips and techniques:

Understand your audience: Knowing your audience is essential to crafting a story that resonates with them. Consider their age, gender, cultural background, and interests.

Develop a strong concept: A great story begins with a strong concept that is unique, memorable, and relevant to your audience. Think about the message you want to convey and how you can do it in an entertaining and engaging way.

Use conflict to create tension: A story without conflict is dull and uninteresting. To make your story more engaging, introduce conflict early on and build tension throughout the narrative.

Show, don't tell: A powerful story is one that engages the audience's senses, emotions, and imagination. Use vivid descriptions, dialogue, and actions to show the story rather than telling it.

Develop characters that the audience can relate to: A compelling story often has well-developed characters that the audience can empathize with. Create characters that have depth, flaws, and aspirations.

Use humor: Humor is an effective tool for engaging the audience and keeping them interested in the story. Use it wisely and appropriately to avoid detracting from the narrative.

Practice, practice, practice: The more you practice storytelling, the better you will become. Seek feedback from others and take note of what works and what doesn't.

To illustrate how these tips can be applied in practice, let's take a look at the movie "The Lion King." The film is a great example of creative storytelling that has captivated audiences of all ages.

The story revolves around Simba, a young lion who must overcome adversity and take his place as king of the Pride Lands. The film uses a strong concept - the circle of life - to convey a powerful message about the importance of responsibility and leadership.

The film introduces conflict early on with the death of Simba's father, Mufasa, and builds tension throughout the narrative as Simba struggles to come to terms with his role as king. The characters are well-developed and relatable, with Simba's journey serving as a metaphor for personal growth and maturity.

The film also uses humor to balance out the drama and keep the audience engaged. The musical numbers, comedic characters, and witty dialogue provide moments of levity amidst the more serious themes of the film.

In conclusion, creative storytelling is an essential skill for any aspiring filmmaker or storyteller. By following these tips and studying examples like "The Lion King," you can learn how to craft compelling narratives that resonate with your audience and leave a lasting impact.

COMMON TYPES OF DOCUMENTARIES EXPLAINED

Here are some common types of documentaries along with suggested interview questions and filming techniques:

Historical documentaries: These documentaries explore a particular period or event in history and often use archival footage and interviews with experts or eyewitnesses.

Interview questions:

What was your experience during this historical event?

How did this event shape your life or the lives of others?

What were the major challenges faced during this time?

Filming techniques:

Use archival footage and photographs to visually represent the time period or event.

Film interviews with experts or eyewitnesses in relevant locations or settings.

Investigative documentaries: These documentaries seek to uncover a particular issue or controversy and often involve extensive research and interviews with key players.

Interview questions:

What is your involvement in this issue or controversy?

How do you think this issue affects society as a whole?

What are the major obstacles to addressing this issue?

Filming techniques:

Use hidden cameras or other undercover techniques to capture footage in relevant locations or settings.

Film interviews with key players in the controversy or issue.

Biographical documentaries: These documentaries focus on the life and career of a particular person, often a public figure or celebrity.

Interview questions:

What were the major challenges you faced in your life or career?

What motivates you to keep going?

What is your legacy or impact on society?

Filming techniques:

Film interviews with the subject and others who knew them well.

Nature documentaries: These documentaries explore the natural world and its inhabitants, often focusing on a particular species or ecosystem.

Interview questions:

What are the major threats to this species or ecosystem?

How can we protect and preserve this environment for future generations?

What are the most interesting or unique aspects of this species or ecosystem?

Filming techniques:

Use time-lapse or slow-motion techniques to capture the movements of animals or natural phenomena.

Film in natural settings at different times of day to capture different lighting and moods.

Social issue documentaries: These documentaries explore a particular social issue or problem, often with the goal of raising awareness and inspiring action.

Interview questions:

What are the root causes of this social issue?

How has this issue affected individuals and communities?

What can we do to address this issue?

Filming techniques:

Film in relevant locations or settings to visually represent the social issue or problem.
Use personal stories and interviews to humanize the issue and connect with viewers emotionally.
Documentary Editing Worksheet:

Identify the main theme or message of your documentary.
Review all of the footage you have filmed and organize it into different categories or sequences.
Create a rough cut of the documentary, focusing on the most important or interesting footage.
Review the rough cut and identify areas that need to be expanded or clarified.
Add additional footage or interviews to fill in gaps or provide more context.
Edit the documentary for pacing and coherence, making sure the story flows logically and is engaging to watch.
Add music, sound effects, and other post-production elements to enhance the mood and tone of the documentary.
Finalize the documentary by color grading, mastering, and exporting it to the desired format.

UNDERSTANDING VISUAL GRAMMER AND FORMATING A SCREEN PLAY AND COMING UP WITH IDEAS FOR YOUR FILM

Class Title: Introduction to Visual Grammar, Mis en scene / Screenwriting - Formatting a screenplay and Generating ideas

Class Objective: The aim of this class is to provide an introduction to visual grammar and mise en scene in film, as well as an overview of the basics of screenwriting, including formatting and generating ideas.

Class Duration: 2 hours

Materials Needed:

Whiteboard or flipchart with markers
Handouts on screenplay formatting and idea generation
Examples of films for visual grammar analysis
Class Outline:

I. Introduction (10 minutes)

Welcome students and introduce class objectives
Explain the importance of visual grammar and mise en scene in film
Explain the basics of screenwriting and why it's important to format a screenplay correctly
II. Visual Grammar and Mise en Scene (40 minutes)

Define visual grammar and explain how it relates to film
Introduce the concept of mise en scene and its importance in film
Analyze examples of films to identify and discuss visual grammar and mise en scene
Discuss how visual grammar and mise en scene can be used to enhance the storytelling in a film
III. Screenwriting - Formatting a Screenplay (30 minutes)

Explain the basics of screenplay formatting, including margins, spacing, and font
Discuss the importance of proper formatting in conveying

information to producers, directors, and actors
Provide examples of correct screenplay formatting and ask students to practice formatting a short scene on their own

IV. Screenwriting - Generating Ideas (30 minutes)

Discuss the importance of idea generation in the screenwriting process
Introduce techniques for generating ideas, such as brainstorming and freewriting
Provide handouts with prompts for idea generation and ask students to generate their own ideas for a short film or scene

V. Conclusion (10 minutes)

Recap the main points covered in the class
Encourage students to continue practicing visual grammar analysis, screenplay formatting, and idea generation on their own

Worksheet:

Title: Visual Grammar Analysis

Instructions: Choose a scene from a film and analyze its visual grammar and mise en scene. Write down your observations in the space provided.

Film: _____

Scene: _____

Observations:

What is the dominant color scheme in the scene?
How is lighting used to create mood or atmosphere?
What is the camera angle and how does it affect the viewer's perspective?
How are the actors framed in the shot and what does this convey about their characters?
What props or set design elements are present and how do they contribute to the scene's meaning?
Title: Idea Generation

Instructions: Use the prompts below to generate your own ideas for a short film or scene. Write down your ideas in the space provided.

Prompts:

A character discovers a mysterious object
Two friends have a falling out over a misunderstanding
A person's mundane routine is interrupted by a surprising event
Ideas:

UNDERSTANDING BLOCKING AND A DIRECTOR FRAMING A SHOT OR SCENE IN A FILM.

Class Title: Filmmaking Fundamentals

Class Description:
This course is designed to provide an introduction to the essential elements of filmmaking. Through lectures, demonstrations, and hands-on exercises, students will learn the fundamental concepts of directing, screenwriting, and camera operation. This course is perfect for anyone interested in pursuing a career in film or those who simply want to gain a better understanding of the craft.

Class Outline:

Week 1 - Director's Craft Exercise Review, Coverage & Blocking

Introduction to the role of the director in filmmaking
The importance of coverage and blocking
Review of a director's craft exercise
Hands-on exercise: blocking and directing a scene
Week 2 - Screenwriting - Writing the Short Narrative, the Outline

Introduction to the art of screenwriting
The three-act structure
Writing a short narrative screenplay
Creating an outline for a short film
Week 3 - Camera - Composition and Lighting

Introduction to the camera and its various components
Understanding composition and framing
Lighting techniques and their impact on the visual style of a film
Hands-on exercise: composition and lighting practice
Week 4 - Practicum: Composition and Lighting Exercise

Review of camera and lighting techniques covered in previous classes
Hands-on exercise: planning and executing a short film scene

with emphasis on composition and lighting
Critique and review of final exercise
Worksheets:

Worksheet 1 - Director's Craft Exercise Review

Review a short film scene and identify the coverage and blocking used
Write a brief analysis of the scene and the director's choices
Worksheet 2 - Screenwriting Outline

Choose a concept for a short film
Write a brief outline using the three-act structure
Worksheet 3 - Composition and Lighting Exercise

Choose a scene from a film and analyze the composition and lighting used
Plan and execute a short film scene using similar techniques
Examples:

Example 1 - Director's Craft Exercise Review
Watch a short film scene and analyze the coverage and blocking used. In a brief analysis, identify the director's choices and how they impact the scene's overall effectiveness.

Example 2 - Screenwriting Outline
Choose a concept for a short film and create a brief outline using the three-act structure. Identify the protagonist, antagonist, and key plot points.

Example 3 - Composition and Lighting Exercise
Analyze a scene from a film and identify the composition and lighting techniques used. Plan and execute a short film scene using similar techniques, and review the final product with the class.

Overall, this course will provide students with a solid foundation in the essential elements of filmmaking. By the end of the course, students will have gained valuable experience and knowledge that they can apply to future projects in the industry.

HOW TO COMPOSE AND FRAME A SHOT FOR A NARRATIVE

Class Title: Camera Techniques and Pre-Production for Short Narrative Films

Introduction:
This class will focus on camera techniques, pre-production, and working with actors and crew for short narrative films. We will cover different camera lenses, composition and lighting, script markup, storyboards, and other pre-production techniques that can help bring a director's vision to life.

Lesson 1: Camera - Composition and Lighting Exercise Review

Review the previous class's composition and lighting exercise and discuss the strengths and weaknesses of each student's work.
Introduce new techniques for composition and lighting that can be applied to short narrative films.
Give students a new exercise to practice their skills.
Worksheet: Camera - Composition and Lighting Exercise

Students will be given a scene to shoot with specific composition and lighting instructions.
Students will shoot the scene and submit their work for review.
Lesson 2: Camera - Lenses

Introduce the different types of camera lenses and how they can be used to achieve specific effects.
Discuss the advantages and disadvantages of different lenses and how to choose the right lens for a shot.
Worksheet: Camera Lenses

Students will be given a list of shots and asked to choose the appropriate lens for each shot.
Lesson 3: Working with Actors

Discuss the director's role in working with actors and how to get the best performances out of them.

Introduce different techniques for directing actors, including character analysis, rehearsals, and improvisation.
Worksheet: Working with Actors

Students will be given a scene and asked to direct actors in a rehearsal.
Lesson 4: Working with Crew

Discuss the importance of pre-production and working with crew to achieve the director's vision.
Introduce different roles in the film crew and their responsibilities.
Discuss techniques for communication and collaboration on set.
Worksheet: Working with Crew

Students will be given a scene and asked to create a shot list and assign roles to the crew.
Lesson 5: Script Markup

Discuss the importance of script markup and how it can help with pre-production and on set.
Introduce different techniques for script markup, including shot lists, camera angles, and blocking.
Worksheet: Script Markup

Students will be given a scene and asked to create a shot list and mark up the script with camera angles and blocking.
Lesson 6: Storyboards

Discuss the importance of storyboards and how they can help with pre-visualization and communication on set.
Introduce different techniques for storyboarding, including sketching and using software.
Worksheet: Storyboards

Students will be given a scene and asked to create storyboards for each shot.
Practicum: Short Narrative Film Exercise

Students will be given a script and asked to plan, shoot, and edit a short narrative film using the techniques learned in the

class.
The film should be no longer than 5 minutes and will be presented and critiqued in class.

Conclusion:
By the end of this class, students will have learned essential techniques for camera work, pre-production, and working with actors and crew for short narrative films. They will have also completed a short film that showcases their skills and creativity.

UNDERSTANDING LOGLINES AND SYNPOSIS IN FILM?

Class: Writer's Toolkit - Introduction, Loglines, Synopsis

Overview:
This class is designed to introduce students to the fundamental tools and techniques of screenwriting. Students will learn how to craft a logline and synopsis that effectively communicate their story to potential readers or producers. They will also explore the key elements of story structure and character development that are essential to creating a successful screenplay.

Objectives:

Understand the key components of a logline and synopsis
Learn how to write a logline and synopsis that effectively communicate a story
Gain an understanding of story structure and character development
Develop critical thinking and analysis skills through reading and analyzing sample loglines and synopses
Lesson Plan:

I. Introduction

Welcome students and introduce the course objectives and goals
Provide an overview of the importance of loglines and synopses in the screenwriting process
Provide examples of successful loglines and synopses from popular films
II. Loglines

Define what a logline is and its importance
Provide examples of effective loglines from films
Discuss the key components of a logline (protagonist, goal, obstacle)
Instruct students to write their own logline for a given prompt or a personal project

Review and provide feedback on student loglines

III. Synopses

Define what a synopsis is and its importance
Provide examples of effective synopses from films
Discuss the key components of a synopsis (protagonist, goal, obstacle, turning points)
Instruct students to write their own synopsis for a given prompt or a personal project
Review and provide feedback on student synopses

IV. Story Structure and Character Development

Discuss the basic elements of story structure (inciting incident, plot points, climax, resolution)
Provide examples of character development from films
Instruct students to analyze and deconstruct the story structure and character development of a given film
Review and discuss the analysis as a group

V. Conclusion

Recap the key elements covered in the class
Encourage students to continue developing their loglines, synopses, and storytelling skills
Provide resources for further study and practice

Worksheets:

Logline template
Synopsis template
Sample loglines and synopses from popular films for analysis

Example:

Prompt: A young woman moves to a small town to start a new life, but discovers a dark secret hidden beneath the surface.

Logline: A young woman seeking a fresh start in a small town uncovers a sinister conspiracy threatening to destroy the community she's come to love.

Synopsis: After a devastating breakup, Emma decides to leave the city behind and start over in the quiet town of Millville. But as she settles into her new life, strange things begin to happen:

unexplained disappearances, cryptic messages, and an ever-present sense of unease. With the help of a local journalist, Emma uncovers a dark secret at the heart of Millville, one that threatens to tear the town apart. Now, she must race against time to uncover the truth before it's too late.

WHAT IS AND ACT AND A THEME WHEN CREATING A MOVIE?

Class Title: Intro to Three Act Structure + Themes

Class Description: This class will introduce the concept of the Three Act Structure in storytelling and explore various themes that can be incorporated into a narrative. Through lectures, discussions, and interactive exercises, students will gain a deeper understanding of the fundamental principles of storytelling.

Lesson Plan:

I. Introduction (15 minutes)

Instructor introduces themselves and explains the objectives of the class
Instructor explains the importance of storytelling and how it can impact audiences
Students introduce themselves and share their interests in storytelling
II. Three Act Structure (60 minutes)

Instructor explains the Three Act Structure and its components (Act I, Act II, Act III)
Instructor shows examples of movies that follow the Three Act Structure
Students discuss how the Three Act Structure can be applied to different types of stories
Students break into groups and identify the Three Act Structure in a popular movie and present their findings to the class
III. Themes in Storytelling (60 minutes)

Instructor introduces common themes in storytelling (e.g. love, redemption, power, family, etc.)
Students discuss examples of movies that incorporate these themes and analyze how they enhance the story
Students break into groups and brainstorm their own story ideas based on a specific theme
Each group presents their story idea and how they incorporated

the theme into their narrative
IV. Conclusion (15 minutes)

Instructor summarizes the key points of the class
Students reflect on what they have learned and how they plan to apply it to their own storytelling
Instructor gives students a homework assignment to write a logline and a brief synopsis for a short film that incorporates the Three Act Structure and a specific theme
Worksheets:

Three Act Structure Worksheet: This worksheet will help students identify the components of the Three Act Structure in a movie and analyze how it impacts the story.

Theme Brainstorming Worksheet: This worksheet will help students brainstorm story ideas based on a specific theme and incorporate it into their narrative.

Logline and Synopsis Worksheet: This worksheet will guide students through the process of creating a logline and a brief synopsis for a short film that incorporates the Three Act Structure and a specific theme.

WHAT ARE ACTS IN A FILM AND HOW TO STUCTURE THEM

The Three-Act Structure is a widely used storytelling technique in film and literature. It is a framework that divides a narrative into three parts: the setup, confrontation, and resolution. Each act has a specific purpose in advancing the story and developing the characters.

Act 1 is the setup, where the audience is introduced to the characters, setting, and main conflict. This act establishes the tone of the story and sets up the main character's goal or objective.

Act 2 is the confrontation, where the main character faces obstacles and challenges that prevent them from achieving their goal. This act is the longest and the most complex, where the story reaches its climax.

Act 3 is the resolution, where the main character confronts the main conflict and resolves it. This act provides closure to the story and ties up any loose ends.

The Three-Act Structure is a useful tool for writers to ensure their story has a clear and satisfying structure. It helps writers avoid common pitfalls like a lack of conflict, a weak climax, or an unsatisfying resolution.

Themes are also an essential aspect of storytelling, and they are the underlying ideas that give a story its meaning. Themes can be universal, like love, betrayal, or sacrifice, or specific to the story's context.

Incorporating themes in a story can help give it depth and resonance, and can also make it more relatable to the audience. Themes can be expressed through character arcs, dialogue, and symbolism.

Overall, understanding the Three-Act Structure and incorporating themes in a story can help writers create compelling and meaningful stories that resonate with their audience.

WHAT IS A LOGLINE AND SYNPOSIS FOR A FILM

Logline and synopsis are two important elements in the process of creating and pitching a film.

A logline is a one or two sentence summary of the main idea or concept of a film. It should be concise and compelling, giving the reader a clear idea of what the film is about, and what makes it unique or interesting. A good logline should also convey the tone and genre of the film, as well as hint at the central conflict or theme.

For example, the logline for the film "Jaws" could be: "A small town sheriff teams up with a marine biologist and a fisherman to hunt down a man-eating great white shark terrorizing the community."

A synopsis, on the other hand, is a more detailed summary of the film's plot, characters, and themes. It can range from a few paragraphs to several pages in length, and is often used to pitch the film to producers, investors, or studios. A good synopsis should include the key story beats, character arcs, and major conflicts of the film, as well as highlighting the themes and tone.

For example, the synopsis for "Jaws" could include a summary of the opening scene, in which a young woman is attacked and killed by the shark, the introduction of the main characters, their initial skepticism about the threat posed by the shark, and the escalating tension and danger as they attempt to hunt it down. It could also highlight the themes of fear, heroism, and the destructive power of nature.

CHARACTER AND CHARACTER TYPES EXPLAINED FOR FILM AND TV SHOWS

Class: Characters in Film and Television

Introduction:
Characters are an essential part of storytelling in film and television. They are the driving force of the story and help

connect the audience to the narrative. In this class, we will be exploring the different types of characters, character development, and how to create compelling characters.

Lesson Plan:

Types of Characters:
a. Protagonist
b. Antagonist
c. Supporting Characters
d. Foil Characters
e. Anti-Heroes

Character Development:
a. Backstory
b. Character Arcs
c. Motivations
d. Relationships

Creating Compelling Characters:
a. Character Traits
b. Dialogue
c. Actions
d. Choices
e. Flaws

Examples of Memorable Characters:
a. Indiana Jones (Indiana Jones series)
b. Hannibal Lecter (The Silence of the Lambs)
c. Tony Stark/Iron Man (Marvel Cinematic Universe)
d. Walter White (Breaking Bad)
e. Daenerys Targaryen (Game of Thrones)

Worksheets:

Character Development Worksheet:
a. Name:
b. Backstory:
c. Motivations:
d. Relationships:
e. Character Arc:

Creating Compelling Characters Worksheet:
a. Character Traits:
b. Dialogue:
c. Actions:
d. Choices:
e. Flaws:

Memorable Characters Analysis Worksheet:
a. Character Name:
b. Movie/TV Show:
c. Character Traits:
d. Dialogue:
e. Actions:
f. Choices:
g. Flaws:
h. Why is this character memorable?

Conclusion:
By the end of this class, you will have a solid understanding of the different types of characters, how to develop them, and how to create compelling and memorable characters. Remember, characters are an essential part of storytelling, and understanding them is crucial for successful filmmaking and television production.

HOW TO WRITE A SCENE FOR LIVE ACTION OR CGI FILM

Class Title: Writing Scenes for Film and Television

Overview: This class will focus on the fundamentals of writing scenes for film and television. Students will learn how to create dynamic and engaging scenes that advance the plot, reveal character, and evoke emotion in the audience. We will explore different genres of film and television, including live action, CGI film, 2D cartoon, romance, action, drama, and thriller. By the end of the class, students will have a solid understanding of scene structure and how to create compelling scenes that capture the audience's attention.

Lesson Plan:

Introduction to Scene Writing (30 minutes)

Definition of a scene
Purpose of a scene
Elements of a scene
Different types of scenes
Scene Structure (60 minutes)

Introduction to the three-act structure
The role of scenes in the three-act structure
The structure of a scene
Scene beats and how they advance the plot
Writing Scenes for Different Genres (90 minutes)

Writing scenes for live action films
Writing scenes for CGI films
Writing scenes for 2D cartoons
Writing romantic scenes
Writing action scenes
Writing dramatic scenes
Writing thriller scenes
Scene Exercise (60 minutes)

Students will work on writing a scene for their chosen genre
Students will share their scenes with the class for feedback
Scene Analysis (60 minutes)

Analyzing scenes from popular films and television shows
Discussing how the scenes were written and structured
Conclusion (30 minutes)

Recap of the key takeaways from the class
Final questions and discussion
Worksheets:

Scene Structure Worksheet - students will use this worksheet to identify the key elements of a scene and its structure.
Scene Analysis Worksheet - students will use this worksheet to analyze and deconstruct scenes from popular films and

television shows.
Scene Exercise Worksheet - students will use this worksheet to plan and write a scene for their chosen genre.
Examples:

Live Action Film - A tense, action-packed scene where the hero is chased by the villain through a crowded city street.
CGI Film - A magical scene where the protagonist discovers a hidden world inside a tree, filled with glowing mushrooms and mythical creatures.
2D Cartoon - A funny scene where the main character tries to catch a mouse in their house, but hilariously fails every time.
Romance - A romantic scene where the two main characters confess their love for each other in a beautiful, scenic location.
Action - A thrilling scene where the hero fights off multiple enemies in an intense, hand-to-hand combat sequence.
Drama - A heart-wrenching scene where a character has a difficult conversation with a loved one about their illness.
Thriller - A suspenseful scene where the protagonist is stalked by an unknown figure in a dark alley.

HOW TO CREATE A SAMPLE SCENE AND DIALOGUE FOR A MOVIE

Class Title: Introduction to Scene Writing and Dialogue

Class Objective: In this class, students will learn how to write effective scenes for films by exploring character development, scene structure, and dialogue. They will also learn how to create a character breakdown and use it to write a sample scene.

Materials Needed:

Pen and paper
A writing software program (such as Final Draft or Celtx)
Class Outline:

I. Introduction

Briefly discuss the importance of scene writing and dialogue
Explain the class objectives and activities
II. Character Breakdown

Discuss the importance of creating a character breakdown
Review a sample character breakdown
Have students create their own character breakdown
III. Sample Scene Writing

Discuss the basic structure of a scene
Review a sample scene and analyze it for structure and character development
Have students write their own sample scene using the character breakdown they created in the previous activity
IV. Dialogue

Discuss the purpose and importance of dialogue
Review a sample scene and analyze the dialogue for subtext and character development
Have students practice writing dialogue for their own sample scene
V. Conclusion

Review the key points covered in the class
Provide resources for further learning
Worksheets:

Character Breakdown Worksheet: This worksheet will guide students through the process of creating a character breakdown, including physical attributes, personality traits, and character goals.

Sample Scene Writing Worksheet: This worksheet will provide students with a template for writing a sample scene, including scene headings, action lines, and dialogue.

Dialogue Writing Worksheet: This worksheet will guide students through the process of writing effective dialogue, including subtext, character voice, and pacing.

Example Scene:

Title: "The Interview"

Characters:

Lisa (mid-20s, nervous, trying to impress)
Mark (late-30s, stern, intimidating)
Synopsis: Lisa is interviewing for her dream job at a law firm, but the interviewer, Mark, seems less than impressed with her credentials. As the interview progresses, Lisa becomes increasingly desperate to impress him, leading to a tense confrontation.

Sample Scene:

INT. LAW FIRM - DAY

Lisa sits across from Mark at a conference table, fidgeting with her hands.

MARK
So, Lisa, tell me about your experience in criminal law.

LISA
(stammering) Well, um, I interned at a public defender's office

during law school, and I also volunteered with a local nonprofit that provides legal services to low-income individuals.

Mark raises an eyebrow.

MARK
And that's it?

Lisa's face falls.

LISA
(defeated) Yes, that's all.

Mark leans forward, his eyes boring into hers.

MARK
Do you know how many applicants we get for this position? Do you have any idea how competitive it is?

Lisa gulps.

LISA
(tentatively) I understand, but I'm willing to work hard and learn.

Mark leans back in his chair, studying her.

MARK
(softening slightly) Look, Lisa, I'll be honest with you. You don't have the experience we're looking for. But there's something about you that intrigues me.

Lisa sits up straighter, hopeful.

MARK
(continuing) So here's what I'm going to do. I'm going to give you a chance. But you need to prove yourself. Can you handle that?

Lisa nods, determined.

LISA
Yes, sir. I won't let you down.

Mark stands up, extending his hand.

MARK
Welcome to the team, Lisa.

Lisa beams, shaking his hand

PREPARING A CLASS ON LEARNING DIALOGUE IN FILMMAKING PROCRESS

Class Title: Dialogue and Subtext in Filmmaking

Class Description: This class will focus on the importance of dialogue and subtext in film and how they can enhance the storytelling process. Students will learn how to write effective dialogue and use subtext to convey deeper meaning in their scripts. Through analysis of famous film scenes and writing exercises, students will gain a deeper understanding of how dialogue and subtext can bring their characters to life and advance the plot.

Lesson Plan:

I. Introduction

Introduce the topic of dialogue and subtext in filmmaking
Discuss the importance of effective dialogue and subtext in storytelling

II. Analyzing Famous Film Scenes

Analyze famous film scenes to understand how dialogue and subtext are used effectively
Discuss how dialogue and subtext can enhance character development and advance the plot

III. Writing Exercises

Provide writing exercises to help students practice writing effective dialogue and subtext
Have students share their work and receive feedback from the class

IV. Subtext in Action

Discuss how subtext can be used to convey deeper meaning in a scene
Provide examples of subtext in action and how it can enhance the storytelling process

V. Writing Workshop

Have students workshop their scenes and discuss how they can incorporate effective dialogue and subtext into their scripts
Provide feedback and guidance to help students improve their writing

VI. Conclusion

Summarize the importance of effective dialogue and subtext in filmmaking
Encourage students to continue practicing their writing and using these techniques in their future projects
Worksheets:

Analyzing Famous Film Scenes: Students will watch and analyze famous film scenes to understand how dialogue and subtext are used effectively. They will answer questions about the scenes to gain a deeper understanding of how dialogue and subtext can enhance character development and advance the plot.

Writing Exercises: Students will be provided with writing exercises to help them practice writing effective dialogue and subtext. They will be asked to write short scenes and dialogue, incorporating the techniques they have learned in the class.

Subtext in Action: Students will be provided with examples of subtext in action and how it can enhance the storytelling process. They will be asked to analyze the examples and discuss how subtext can be used in their own writing.

Writing Workshop: Students will workshop their scenes and discuss how they can incorporate effective dialogue and subtext into their scripts. They will receive feedback and guidance to help them improve their writing.

Examples:

Example 1:
Scene: A couple is having dinner at a restaurant.

Dialogue:
Him: "How was work today?"
Her: "Fine."
Him: "Just fine? What did you do?"
Her: "The usual. Meetings, emails, reports."
Him: "Anything interesting happen?"
Her: "Not really."

Subtext:
The woman is clearly hiding something from her partner. Her short, dismissive answers suggest that she doesn't want to talk about her day. This creates tension in the scene and suggests that there is a deeper issue in their relationship.

Example 2:
Scene: A detective is interrogating a suspect.

Dialogue:
Detective: "Where were you on the night of the murder?"
Suspect: "I don't remember."
Detective: "Try harder. We have evidence that puts you at the scene of the crime."
Suspect: "I don't know what you're talking about."
Detective: "You're lying. Why don't you just confess?"

Subtext:
The detective is using the evidence to pressure the suspect into confessing, but the suspect is denying any involvement. This creates a sense of tension and suspense in the scene, as the audience is unsure whether the suspect is telling the truth or not. The subtext suggests that

HOW TO PREPARE A CLASS ON TEACHING BEAT SHEETS

Class: Turning Points and Beat Sheets in Film Production

Objectives:

To understand the concept of turning points and their importance in storytelling.
To learn how to use beat sheets to structure a screenplay.
To practice identifying turning points and creating beat sheets for film projects.
Materials:

Whiteboard and markers
Handouts on turning points and beat sheets
Samples of beat sheets from popular films
Writing prompts for creating beat sheets
Lesson:

Introduction (10 minutes)
Discuss the importance of turning points in storytelling and their impact on the audience.
Introduce the concept of beat sheets as a tool for structuring a screenplay.
Turning Points (20 minutes)
Define what a turning point is and discuss its significance in a story.
Use examples from popular films to illustrate different types of turning points (e.g. inciting incident, midpoint, climax).
Have students identify turning points in a film clip or short story.
Beat Sheets (20 minutes)
Introduce the concept of a beat sheet and its purpose in structuring a screenplay.
Discuss the elements of a beat sheet (e.g. acts, sequences, scenes).
Show samples of beat sheets from popular films and analyze their structure.
Practice (30 minutes)

Divide students into pairs or small groups.
Provide writing prompts for creating beat sheets for different genres (e.g. action, romance, drama).
Have students share their beat sheets and discuss how they structured their stories.
Conclusion (10 minutes)
Review the key concepts of turning points and beat sheets.
Encourage students to continue practicing their skills in identifying turning points and creating beat sheets.
Worksheets:

Turning Points Worksheet:
A list of questions to help students identify turning points in a story or film clip.
Space for students to write down their answers and analyze the impact of each turning point on the story.
Beat Sheet Template:
A blank template for students to create their own beat sheets. Includes sections for acts, sequences, and scenes, as well as prompts for identifying turning points and writing notes on subplots and character arcs.

HOW TO PREPARE A CLASS ON TEACHING DIALOGUE AND SUBTEXT

Class: Dialogue and Subtext Exercise Review

Objective: In this class, we will review and analyze a previously written dialogue scene to understand the subtext and deeper meaning behind the characters' words. This will help us better understand how to write impactful and meaningful dialogue in our own screenplays.

Materials:

A previously written dialogue scene
Worksheets for analyzing dialogue and subtext
Procedure:

Introduction to Subtext: Begin by defining subtext in dialogue and its importance in screenwriting. Explain that subtext is the underlying meaning behind what characters say, and that it is often more important than the actual words spoken.

Scene Analysis: Hand out the previously written dialogue scene to the class. Have the class read through the scene and identify the main points of dialogue and the characters' intentions.

Subtext Analysis: Using the worksheets, guide the class through analyzing the subtext of the dialogue. Encourage students to look for hidden meanings, character motivations, and underlying emotions that are not explicitly stated in the dialogue.

Character Breakdown: Have the class analyze each character in the scene, looking at their motivations, desires, and how they are using subtext to communicate with the other character.

Group Discussion: Lead a group discussion on the scene, analyzing the subtext and how it contributes to the overall story. Encourage students to share their insights and interpretations of the scene.

Writing Exercise: Have students write their own dialogue scene, using the techniques and insights they learned from analyzing the previous scene.

Scene Review: Review the scenes written by students and analyze them for subtext and effective use of dialogue.

Conclusion: Wrap up the class by summarizing the importance of subtext in dialogue and how it can be used to create more impactful and meaningful scenes.

Worksheets:

Worksheet 1: Dialogue Analysis

Identify the main points of dialogue in the scene.
Analyze the tone and mood of the scene.

Identify the emotions expressed by each character.
Worksheet 2: Subtext Analysis

Identify the underlying meaning behind the dialogue.
Analyze the character motivations and desires.
Identify the subtextual cues used by the characters.
Worksheet 3: Character Breakdown

Analyze each character's motivations, desires, and backstory.
Identify how each character is using subtext to communicate.
Analyze the power dynamic between the characters.

EXERCISE FOR BEAT SHEET FOR STUDENTS

Class Title: Beat Sheet Exercise for Filmmaking

Overview: In this class, students will learn about the importance of beat sheets in the screenwriting process and how to create a beat sheet for a film. They will also participate in a beat sheet exercise to practice their skills.

Materials Needed:

Whiteboard and markers
Handouts with examples of beat sheets
Pen and paper for students
Lesson Plan:

I. Introduction (15 minutes)

Explain to students what a beat sheet is and its importance in the screenwriting process.
Discuss the three-act structure and how beat sheets are used to organize the plot.
Provide examples of beat sheets from popular films such as "The Dark Knight" and "Star Wars."
II. Creating a Beat Sheet (30 minutes)

Instruct students to choose a film they are familiar with and create a beat sheet for it.
Provide a template or guide for students to follow, including key

plot points and turning points.
Encourage students to consider the themes and character arcs of the film as they create their beat sheet.
III. Beat Sheet Exercise (60 minutes)

Divide students into small groups.
Assign each group a film and provide them with a beat sheet that has key plot points removed.
Instruct students to work together to fill in the missing plot points and create a complete beat sheet for the film.
After the exercise, each group will present their beat sheet to the class.
IV. Discussion and Reflection (15 minutes)

Lead a class discussion on the importance of beat sheets in the screenwriting process.
Ask students to reflect on what they learned from the exercise and how they can apply it to their own writing.
Worksheets:

Example Beat Sheets: Handouts with examples of beat sheets from popular films.
Beat Sheet Template: A template or guide for students to follow when creating their own beat sheet.
Homework:

Instruct students to create a beat sheet for their own film idea, using the template provided in class.

WHAT IS A BEAT SHEET?

Welcome to the Beat Sheet Review and Refinement class for new filmmakers!

Today, we will be reviewing and refining the beat sheets for your film projects. A beat sheet is a tool used by screenwriters to break down a story into its essential plot points, which are then used to structure the script. The beat sheet can be a valuable tool to help you stay on track and ensure that your story has a clear and compelling narrative arc.

Let's begin with a review of the basic structure of a beat sheet. A traditional beat sheet is divided into three acts, with each act containing specific plot points:

Act I:

Opening Image
Theme Stated
Set-Up
Catalyst
Debate

Act II:

Break into Two
B Story
Fun and Games
Midpoint
Bad Guys Close In
All Is Lost
Dark Night of the Soul

Act III:

Break into Three
Finale
Final Image

Now, let's take a look at your beat sheets. Take a moment to read through them and identify any areas that you feel are unclear or weak. Are there any plot points that seem out of place or unnecessary? Are there any plot holes or inconsistencies that need to be addressed?

Next, we will work on refining your beat sheets. One technique you can use is to focus on the character arc of your protagonist. Does the plot of your film allow your protagonist to experience growth and change over the course of the story? If not, you may need to rework your beat sheet to ensure that the protagonist has a clear and compelling journey.

Another technique is to focus on the themes of your story. Are there any themes that emerge from your beat sheet? Are these themes strong and consistent throughout the story? If not, you may need to revisit your beat sheet and work on integrating your themes more effectively.

Now, let's turn to a group exercise. In pairs or small groups, exchange your beat sheets and offer constructive feedback to one another. Use the structure we have reviewed today to identify areas of strength and weakness in each other's beat sheets, and work together to refine and improve them.

Finally, take a moment to reflect on what you have learned today. How can you apply these skills and techniques to your own writing and filmmaking projects in the future? Remember, a well-crafted beat sheet can be a valuable tool to help you stay on track and tell a compelling story. With practice and dedication, you can hone your skills and become a skilled storyteller.

WHAT SHOULD BE INCLUDED IN EACH ACT OF YOUR FILM?

Opening Image
Theme Stated
Set-Up
Catalyst
Debate
Act II:

Break into Two
B Story
Fun and Games
Midpoint
Bad Guys Close In
All Is Lost
Dark Night of the Soul
Act III:

Break into Three
Finale
Final Image
ChatGPT

Sure, here is a detailed explanation of each act in a beat sheet, along with examples and worksheets:

ACT I:

Opening Image: This is the first image that the audience sees on screen, which sets the tone for the entire story. It should be visually striking and give a glimpse into the world of the story.

Example: The opening shot of "The Godfather" shows a man asking for a favor from the Godfather, establishing the world of organized crime and power struggles.

Worksheet: Write a one-sentence description of your opening image and how it sets the tone for your story.

Theme Stated: This is where the central theme of the story is introduced, either through dialogue or action.

Example: In "Star Wars", the theme is introduced when Luke Skywalker longs for a life beyond his mundane existence, setting up the story of his journey to become a hero.

Worksheet: Write down the central theme of your story and how it will be introduced in the Theme Stated section.

Set-Up: This is where the audience is introduced to the main characters, their relationships, and the world they inhabit.

Example: In "The Matrix", the audience is introduced to Neo's mundane life as a computer programmer, his relationship with Morpheus, and the mysterious world of the Matrix.

Worksheet: Write down the main characters in your story, their relationships, and the world they inhabit.

Catalyst: This is the event that sets the story in motion, and creates a need for the main character to take action.

Example: In "Jurassic Park", the catalyst is the creation of dinosaurs through genetic engineering, which leads to the need to bring experts to the island to evaluate the safety of the park.

Worksheet: Write down the catalyst event that sets your story in motion.

Debate: This is where the main character struggles with whether or not to take action, often due to fear or uncertainty.

Example: In "The Lord of the Rings: The Fellowship of the Ring", Frodo debates whether to take on the responsibility of the ring, knowing the dangers that come with it.

Worksheet: Write down the main character's internal debate and what factors are causing it.

ACT II:

Break into Two: This is where the main character decides to take action and begins their journey.

Example: In "The Wizard of Oz", Dorothy decides to leave home and follow the yellow brick road to find the Wizard.

Worksheet: Write down the main character's decision to take action and what it means for the story.

B Story: This is the subplot of the story, often involving a romantic interest or a side character's journey.

Example: In "Titanic", the B story is the romantic relationship between Jack and Rose, which is intertwined with the main story of the sinking ship.

Worksheet: Write down the B story of your story and how it connects to the main plot.

Fun and Games: This is the section of the story where the main character faces challenges and has initial successes, often with a sense of excitement and adventure.

Example: In "Indiana Jones and the Raiders of the Lost Ark", the Fun and Games section involves Indiana Jones traveling the world to find the Ark, facing challenges and triumphs along the way.

Worksheet: Write down the challenges and successes that the main character faces in the Fun and Games section.

Midpoint: This is the turning point of the story, where the main character's goals or beliefs are changed.

Example: In "The Hunger Games", the Midpoint involves Katniss realizing that Peeta is not just playing a game in the arena, but truly cares for her and wants to survive with her.

Worksheet: Write down the turning point of your story and how it changes the main character's goals o

Manufactured by Amazon.ca
Bolton, ON

36903565R00101